Tom Thomson's
Fine Kettle of Friends:
biography, history, art and food

"What a delightful book! A great idea! Thank you for doing such excellent work." **Joan Murray**, art historian and Tom Thomson scholar.

"I very much enjoyed reading the text. It is full of interesting tidbits on Thomson's early years and working his life around recipes is great fun." **Charles Hill,** former National Gallery of Canada Curator of Canadian Art.

"Utterly enjoyable reading! The people and places in Tom Thomson's life come alive in Littlefield's richly detailed stories. Truly fabulous." **Nancy Lang,** researcher and co-producer for White Pine Pictures' *West Wind: The Vision of Tom Thomson.*

"I enjoyed the tasty outing with Thomson and Edgar Burke's family on Fairy Lake including a too brief visit with an austere Winnifred Trainor." **Neil Lehto,** author, *Algonquin Elegy: Tom Thomson's Last Spring.*

"It is appropriate that Littlefield devotes an entire chapter to Minnie, Tom's favourite sister. No wonder that Tom, an adventurer himself, favoured this feisty girl who plundered her dowry to enrol in college, studying classics, language, music, art and more – and stuck to it for three years, eventually marrying (after some consideration) at age 32. The accounts of Tom and Minnie's outings give a deep sense of their affection for each other, and their delight in the 'delicious food' served at Tom's favourite McConkey's on King Street." **Amanda Hale,** author, *In the Embrace of the Alligator*, *Sounding the Blood, My Sweet Curiosity* and *The Reddening Path.*

"I'm very impressed with the Archie Belaney chapter: a mix of document-based information with open speculation in a way that is quite compelling. **Dennis Reid,** author, *A Concise History of Canadian Painting,* editor, *Tom Thomson.*

"What struck me was the amazing mobility of the Thomson family and their friends. They were peripheral, or central, to so many endeavours in our young country. Ms. Littlefield has shown us life in early Canada with a much richer palette than we might have imagined. Do join us for dinner!" **Ruth Abernethy,** sculptor and author of *Life and Bronze.*

"Angie Littlefield has brought it all together: Tom Thomson, his history and his life; food and how it used to be and how it brought people together—and Canada with its history, everyday life and spelling. Finally, it's not cutting out letters to save money by using American spelling. This book shows through people and food who we are, because of where we came from." **Rebecca Middleton,** editorial researcher White Pine Pictures, including *West Wind: The Vision of Tom Thomson*.

"I am very impressed with your latest Tom Thomson presentation and offer my humble comments on the outstanding research and writing. You have, again, advanced my writer's inferiority complex. Your book is a real masterpiece with in-depth research and outstanding pictorial support!" **Robert Lavack**, Sweden/Canada, author of "Flying high with Morrisseau", *The Morrisseau Papers, Nun of That* and "sometimes war chooses you".

"This lively book will give the reader a vivid sense of Tom Thomson as a personality beyond his art. Thomson's friendships, in particular with the colourful J.W. Beatty, are wonderfully evoked." **Amy Furness,** Rosamond Ivey Special Archivist & Head, Library & Archives, Art Gallery of Ontario.

"What a wonderful book! It has been a real delight to read. Regardless of how familiar you might feel you are with Tom Thomson and his life, there is a freshness to how Angie Littlefield tells the story. Anyone interested in Thomson, early 19th century life or cooking will definitely enjoy this book." **Virginia Eichhorn,** Director & Chief Curator, Tom Thomson Art Gallery.

"This engagingly written book presents well researched narratives that enhance our understanding of Tom Thomson through facts and possibilities concerning his life. A good example is H.B. "Harry" Jackson accompanying Tom on his first visit to Algonquin in May 1912, a trip which was the initial spark in Thomson's intense artistic love affair with the Park." **Ron Tozer**, Algonquin Park Naturalist (retired) and author of *Birds of Algonquin Park.*

Tom Thomson's Toronto Neighbourhoods*, 2nd edition, 2016

Ilse Salberg: Weimar Photographer*, 2015

The Ten Best Modern Medical Marvels, with Jennifer Littlefield, 2012

Reading and Remembrance**, 2005–2012

Robert's Worst Sheep–Shearing Day, Ever!* And *The Wreck of the MS Oliva*,*
written by the children of Tristan da Cuhna, ed., 2012

Elisapee of the Arctic: Mallikjuak Adventure*, written by the children of Cape Dorset, ed., 2010

angelika hoerle: the comet of cologne dada, 2009

The Art of Dissent: Willy Fick, 2008

The Ten Deadliest Plants, with Jennifer Littlefield, 2007

The Ten Grossest Bugs, with Jennifer Littlefield, 2007

Two of the Talented Thomsons: George Thomson O.S.A. 1868–1965, Margaret Thomson 1884–1979, 2006

The Thomsons of Durham: Tom Thomson's Family Heritage, 2005

The Dada Period in Cologne: Selections from the Fick–Eggert Collection, 1988

*Available free online at angielittlefield.com

**Available free online at readingandremembrance.ca

Permanent member Art Gallery of Ontario, member Writers' Union of Canada

Tom Thomson's Fine Kettle of Friends:
BIOGRAPHY, HISTORY, ART AND FOOD

BY ANGIE LITTLEFIELD

Best Wishes!

Angie Ltd

Table of Contents

To my husband David Littlefield

Marangi Editions
72 Baronial Court
Toronto, ON, Canada M1C 3J7

www.angielittlefield.com

Cataloguing data available from Library and Archives Canada

ISBN 978-0-9958318-0-31.

1. Tom Thomson, biography.

2. Artists John Beatty, J.E.H. MacDonald, Thoreau MacDonald, Franklin Carmichael.

3. Social history Canada 1867–1917.

4. Canadian culinary history 20th century.

5. Algonquin Park.

6. Lumbermen.

Editing by Mary Cook

Copy editing by Rebecca Middleton and Mary Cook

Cover and text design by Mary Cook

Special visuals by Andrea Ketelaars

Includes bibliographic references and index

Disclaimer: Due diligence has been undertaken to acknowledge the sources of images.

Cascadia Author Services

Printed in Canada

AGO–Art Gallery of Ontario

AO–Archives of Ontario, DBS, Donald B. Smith Fonds

APMA–Algonquin Park Museum and Archives

CTA–City of Toronto Archives

GRM–Grey Roots Museum

LAC–Library and Archives Canada

MCAC–McMichael Canadian Art Collection

MHPC–Muskoka Heritage Place Collection

NGC–National Gallery of Canada

PD–Public Domain-works over 75 years old and/or accessible on the internet

SA–Sheffield Archives

TFC–Thomson Family Collection–photographs originating with Kay Morrison and Helen Young, grandnieces of Tom Thomson. Kay is now deceased but was a huge contributor of knowledge and resources for *The Thomsons of Durham: Tom Thomson's Family Heritage.* Helen Young and her family continue to be very helpful contributors.

TPL–Toronto Public Library, Special Collections, SC

TRL–Toronto Reference Library and Virtual Reference, VR

TTMA–Tom Thomson Memorial Art Gallery

TUA–Trent University Archives

WAG–Winnipeg Art Gallery

Top Left: *Main Library, Toronto 1948,* photo, PD.

Left: *Lumber Raft, Ottawa River 1890,* photo, William Notman & Son, 1885–1895, Notman Photographic Archives, McCord Museum.

Top Right: *By the Queen! The Queen's Proclamation of Confederation,* ephemera, PD.

Far Right: *Cyclorama of the Canadian National Exhibition, no. 2, 1909,* photo, PD.

CHAPTER ONE

Introduction to a Culinary Life

rom an early age, Canada's renowned artist Tom Thomson cleaned and cooked the fish he caught in Telfer Creek[i] and off Ainslie's Wharf[ii] in his hometown Leith, near Owen Sound. His mother, Margaret, Aunt Henrietta and five sisters made pies from game he shot. With his four brothers, he harvested the farm's crops of oats, peas, and turnips. He watched his father, John, tend a large kitchen garden. The cooking masters of the family's kitchen taught him to bake, pickle, and make preserves. Each fall he stepped into his father's five-and-a-half-metre-long rowboat[iii] to haul in the salmon trout the family pickled in brine and kept in the basement for the winter.

Then in 1898, when he was 21-years-of-age, Tom left the farm. In Seattle and Toronto, he worked for engraving firms, lived in boarding houses, and dabbled in sketching and painting. He went dancing, fishing, snowshoeing, to films, the Canadian National Exhibition, the Mendelssohn Choir[iv], and boxing matches. He had girlfriends, visited with family, took photographs, and read library books. For 14 years, until he was 35-years-of-age, this was Tom Thomson's life.

That changed in 1912 when Tom Thomson went to Algonquin Park, and further north, never to live the same life again. He grew into his skills as an artist, and captured Canada's north with a new vision. A great deal is written about his art and his mysterious death on Canoe Lake in 1917. Much less is written about his life. I looked further into Tom's life story and found short bursts of praise for his cooking, mostly from family members and colleagues, people with walk-on parts in art history. These small references prompted research into the persons who saw fit to praise Tom's culinary talents.

Who were the men and women who broke bread with Canada's most famous artist?

Tom's friendships yielded rich new material about him, life at the turn of the 20th century and about the newly minted country, Canada.

Tom was born in 1877 when Canada was a mere 10 years old. He grew up when the lumber trade flourished on the Great Lakes and in the Ottawa River Valley. Railroads were expanding, urban centres were undergoing electrification, the graphic arts field was growing and free or cheap land was to be had on the prairies. His generation was leaving small towns by

the thousands, pioneering new fields of endeavour and exploring what it meant to be Canadian.

During these heady, changing times, Tom had meals and engaged in conversation with people from all walks of life. He ate in fine restaurants, on the trail in Ontario's north, and from pots cooked over a wood-burning stove in "The Shack" in Toronto's Rosedale Valley. His various companions included a lumber camp cook, Algonquin Park ranger, a railroad engineer, a sister, graphic artists, future members of the Group of Seven and the greatest fraudster Canada has known, Grey Owl.

The lives of Tom's friends provided vignettes of Canada in its early years as a country; they also proved the adage that you can tell a lot about a man from the company he keeps. When I took the time to look into Tom's use of his cooking kit (long-handled frying pan, Dutch oven, tea kettle, reflector oven, and berry pails), I found a lot more than his interest in good food.

The story of Tom's life as told through his friendships, cooking stories and period recipes, is a story made to mark Canada's 150th anniversary.

Claremont Farm, photo Mary Cook

CHAPTER TWO

Life on the Farm

"*I have never seen people so fond of flowers, and both Mother and Father were. If there was a new kind of rose came out, Father was not happy until he had it in his garden and he had a lovely collection of 21 varieties and all colours, beside all kinds of lovely flowers. Last spring for all he was not in his usual robust health, he put in four hundred gladiolus bulbs and he lived to enjoy the gorgeous blooms in his sick room.*"

Louisa[v] Thomson Henry letter to Blodwen Davies, March 11, 1931

The family of John and Margaret Thomson moved from the rolling hills of Claremont in southern Ontario to a farm in the small hamlet of Leith when John sold the farmlands he'd inherited from his parents.[vi] Tom, their sixth child, was a few months old in the fall of 1877 when the Thomson's long horse-drawn wagon train wended its way up the Sydenham Road[vii] towards Owen Sound. The farm animals plodded behind. John and Margaret would have four more children in Leith.

Rose Hill Farm, Leith Ontario, photo, LAC-C-027133.
Note the enclosed side garden.

John Thomson set about recreating his new bailiwick called Rose Hill Farm as soon as spring broke in his new community. According to the *Tweedsmuir History of Annan,* compiled by the ladies of the Women's Institute, John Thomson added a back extension to the house, improved the water situation by building a cistern, had a new well hand dug, and made alterations to enlarge the outbuildings. He planted an apple orchard in front of the house and laid out a large oval garden beside it. He made sure the garden was tile-drained, filled with rich soil from the back of the farm and enclosed with a high fence. In half of the garden, John planted flowers and shrubs, as he'd loved flower gardens since he was a boy in Claremont. In the other half of his new garden, he set out five rows of grape vines, currant and berry bushes, a rhubarb patch, and strawberry beds. He left space for vegetables.[viii]

As Tom Thomson grew into a boy, he saw that from the first summer yields to the last harvest of fall, the household was about cooking, baking, preserving, and pickling. The processing of foods included maple sugar making, salting meats, drying herbs and fruits, harvesting ice, the winter storage of apples and root vegetables, and the brining of fish. In addition, household members baked their daily bread, churned butter, and husbanded farm animals for milk and meat.

The wilder side of Leith provided fish and game. John Thomson kept a rowboat and a spate of shot guns, rifles, and fishing rods. He was fond of hunting ducks and partridge, and of fly fishing for trout. As a lad, Tom shot squirrels from which the Thomson kitchen produced black squirrel pie. He wore the squirrel tails on a felt hat he shaped over a broom handle.[ix] The fish that the young Tom caught in abundance seldom made it home. He cleaned and smoked them in a length of stovepipe over an open fire. Tom's friend, Allan Ross, told Thomson biographer Blodwen Davies, "He seemed to be one of those people who was born with a shotgun in one hand and a fishing rod in the other."[x]

When Tom was a restless teenager—out of school, but not as he wished to be, a deckhand on the very busy shipping routes of the Great Lakes—he roamed the hills and forests around Leith. Trout was his main goal, but he didn't need to look far for edibles. Nature provided a sampler of wild berries, mushrooms, and greens. Luck must have been with him, as he survived nature's more poisonous offerings—water hemlock often confused with edible wild parsnip and potentially lethal Moonseed which pretended to be wild grapes.

When he turned 21-years-of–age, Tom came into a sizable inheritance from his grandfather[xi] and with it he left the farm. He took away a great deal of his heritage: a love of family, reading, fishing, music, and art.

He also took his vast experience with cooking, baking, preserving, and foraging.

Tom's appreciation of fine food and his ability to produce it, thread their way through his personal narrative.

The Food Connection

To flesh out the cooking and baking references in Tom's life, I searched archives, museums, and vintage cook books. References to squirrel pie presumed you had a cleaned and trussed one from the same place you bought dressed rabbit and partridge. My local supermarkets lacked this section.

Jaffray Rutherford, photo Angie Littlefield.

Since I wanted to know how Tom's squirrel made the transit from freshly shot, to the pot, I went online. I found home videos of hunters brewing squirrel sludge over smoky campfires. That didn't help. Then fate, in the form of a friendly film team from White Pine Pictures, gave me a lead. I'd worked on White Pine's documentary about Tom called *West Wind,* and the company's researcher extraordinaire, Rebecca Middleton, told me about an elderly gent whose ancestors had been neighbours to the Thomsons from 1877 to approximately 1902, when the Thomsons moved away. The Rutherfords and

Thomsons visited each other's homes[xii], went to the same church and shared a threshing machine with other Leith farmers.[xiii] Jaffray Rutherford, who I was to visit, still lived on ancestral Rutherford lands. I hoped he'd have family memories going back to the early 1900s—if not even earlier.

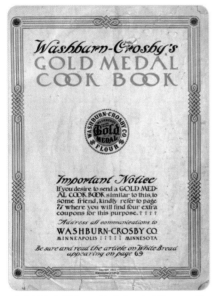

Gold Medal Flour Cook Book, Minneapolis, Washburn-Crosby Co., 1910.

Jaffray Rutherford turned out to be a real charmer. As a bonus, he'd hunted squirrels back in the day. He told me he cleaned them in the same way as a chicken—the chop the head off and tug out the innards type of way. Jaff handed the clean carcasses to his mother who made pies and tarts with them. He didn't remember a particular recipe, but figured it'd be about the same as for any meat pie. Herbs, he said, came from the garden or if they'd been dried, from the cellar. Jaff didn't collect squirrel tails like Tom, but he remembered the coonskin caps boys wore during his growing-up years. To him, tail gathering seemed a boy thing to do.

When I prompted Jaff about baking, his eyes glazed, lost in thought remembering his favourite pie. His mother had baked sour cream pie for him from an old family recipe. That recipe no longer existed. From further queries, I could tell Jaff was the visitor to the kitchen rather than someone like Tom who watched and learned.

I listened to more of Jaff's stories. He and his father had fished from a rowboat, the way Tom had done with his dad and brothers. Jaff's rowboat featured a small kerosene camp stove topped with a heavy pot. He and his dad cleaned the fish, boiled and ate them right in the boat. "Freshest I ever had!" he said.

Jaffray Rutherford loved to speak about the area's history. When he died April 12, 2013, people from far and wide mourned him, as well as the loss of his broad scope of knowledge.

Squirrel Pot Pie from *Gold Medal Flour Cook Book* published by Washburn–Crosby Co., Minnesota, 1910 page 23.

"Squirrels: The large grey and fox squirrels are the best for eating and may be prepared cooked in any way suitable for rabbits.

Squirrel Pot Pie

Prepare squirrels as rabbits, cut in pieces, flour and fry brown in a little good dripping, and place in a stew pan. Add 1 quart boiling water, ¼ of a lemon sliced very thin, a teaspoon of salt, a small glass of sherry and 1 minced onion fried brown in a tablespoon of butter. Cover all closely and stew for an hour. Make a delicate biscuit crust, cut in rounds and lay them on top of the squirrel, let them boil, covered closely, for fifteen minutes; pile the squirrel in the center of a hot platter, arrange dumplings along it. Thicken the gravy with 1 tablespoon of Gold Medal flour browned in 1 tablespoon of butter and pour gravy over meat."

If you'd prefer a Canadian recipe, more suited to Tom Thomson on the trail, here's a 1918 recipe from the Canada Food Board. It's found in *Fancy meats in newest dishes,* page 30. It's described as "rabbit pie", but like the Minnesota recipe, it's good for the bushy-tailed ones. Based on Tom Thomson's extant provisions lists, he'd have substituted salt pork for the pickled pork, and his Dutch oven for the pudding dish. At some point or other, Tom Thomson might even have stewed himself a rabbit.

Rabbit Pie

"1 rabbit, ½ pound pickled pork, 1 cup stock, salt and pepper, crust, onion, herb if desired.

Wash rabbit. Divide into small pieces. Cut pork into dice. Cover all with water and cook until tender. Cool and remove the fat. Place in a pudding dish and cover with oatmeal or potato crust. Onion or herbs may be added during the first cooking."

The recipe ends there without mention of how long the second cooking with crust would take.

Union Depot, Soo, Mich., showing two modes of transportation, by rail and water.

Union Depot, Soo, Michigan, postcard, PD.

By the way, on page 20 of *Fancy meats in newest dishes,* there are recommendations for the use of pork lips and pork ears: "Pork ears are used in the household, boiled with cabbage greens and sauerkraut. In the larger cities in the East, they are used extensively fried or made into sandwiches. They can be used in soups and in making soup stocks."

You know it's Happy 150ᵗʰ Birthday, Canada when you read that the Canada Food Board recommended how to use pigs' ears and lips in menu planning!

Sour Cream Raisin Pie

When I went searching for Jaffray Rutherford's favourite sour cream pie, I found dozens of versions of that recipe, mostly with raisins. They tended to come from a particular family history—a granny or great-granny who had made the pie. Mid-western Mennonites and Norwegians alike claimed the pie as their heritage. It roamed the plains of Kansas and Minnesota. On a Canadian food blog, a lady commented that her 99-year-old grandmother requested her to make the pie as she remembered it from her days working for the Soo Line Railroad in the 1920s. The Soo Line was a Canadian Pacific Railroad subsidiary that linked Minneapolis and Sault Ste. Marie, starting in 1883. Maybe sour cream and raisin pie rode the rails into Canada.

Here's a generic recipe:

Sour Cream and Raisin Pie

2 cups seedless raisins, 2 cups water,
¾ cup granulated sugar, dash of salt,
2 ½ tablespoons corn starch, enough water to
make paste, ½ pint sour cream

Mix raisins, 2 cups water, sugar and salt
together; bring to a boil; stir in corn starch
mixture; cook until clear. Remove from fire; add
sour cream. Pour into unbaked 8 inch pie shell;
add top crust.

Bake in preheated 450F degree oven 10
minutes; reduce heat to 350F and bake until
crust is brown.

Many recipes suggested varying amounts of cinnamon, nutmeg, cloves or vanilla. The seasoning
choices are up to you. The meringue topping was
never considered optional.

*Pickled Pigs Lips, Farm Fresh
Food Suppliers,* label,
Amita, LA, USA

*Well, that's a start to
cooking and baking
150 years ago, the
way Tom Thomson
might have.*

Try it out, but, say no to
pork lips!

The Thomson Siblings

The Thomson Siblings, photos: George excerpt from The Thomson brothers, TFC; Elizabeth LAC-194813; Henry LAC-194805; Louisa LAC-194812; Minnie LAC-194810; Tom LAC-211294; Ralph excerpt from TFC; Margaret LAC-194808; Fraser GRM, PF35854F1I13.

CHAPTER THREE

The Thomson Family Primer

Tom Thomson is frequently imagined as a lone canoeist on a northern lake. Only the call of a loon and the movement of a paddle break the silence. Make room for new images. Tom was a member of a large Scottish-Canadian clan—one of 10 children. The siblings in order of birth were: George, 1868; Elizabeth, 1870; Henry, 1871; Louisa, 1873; Minnie, 1875; Tom, 1877; Ralph, 1880; James, 1882; Margaret (Peggie), 1884; and Fraser, 1886. In addition to this large group, Tom knew well, five of a dozen plus nephews and nieces. He was part of robust family weddings and crowded holidays. Tom Thomson interacted with family members frequently in person, less through letters. Algonquin Park lays claim to Tom Thomson for the last five years of his life. His family has it all. Tom's family provides a context for an artist who was alone on Canoe Lake when he died but never truly alone in life. It's time to meet the family.

The Thomson Family, photo, TFC From left, Henry seated, Tom standing, Elizabeth seated, Minnie standing, George sitting, Ralph standing, Louisa sitting. In front, in white, Fraser standing, Margaret (Peggie) seated.

From birth to 21-years-of-age, Tom was among siblings in Leith. He went to school and church with them; he performed farm chores with them.

Top Left: *Grandfather Thomas "Tam" Thomson (1806–1875),* photo, TFC.

Top Right: *Thomson sisters,* photo, from left Elizabeth, Minnie, Louisa with Margaret in front, TFC.

Lower Left: *Thomson brothers,* photo, from left, Tom, Ralph, George and Henry, TFC.

Lower Right: *Elizabeth Brodie Thomson (1812–1874),* photo, TFC.

Opposite Page: Left: *John Eaton's Catalogue No. 2,* cover, PD.

Right: *Tom Thomson's Mandolin,* Collection of the Tom Thomson Art Gallery, Owen Sound, gift from the Estate of Margaret (Thomson) Tweedale, sister of Tom Thomson, 1980.

Thomson Family Album

A family audience first critiqued his drawings, caricatures and playing of musical instruments. In Seattle, Washington, he was daily with at least one of three brothers as he explored his abilities to do pencil, ink, watercolour and oil sketches. He still regularly visited home in Owen Sound after he started trips to Lake Scugog, Algonquin Park

and the Mississagi River with colleagues from graphic arts firms in Toronto. He caught up with family when he went home first to Leith and then later to Owen Sound when his parents moved there. He sketched them and their surroundings and further honed his artistic skills. The Thomson siblings were much involved in Tom's life, and vice versa.

The stories start with a clarification. The 11th and oldest child in the Thomson's lively household was in fact a cousin. Charlotte Tripp, known as Lottie, was the daughter of Catherine Tripp.[xiv] When Catherine died in childbirth in 1866, Tom's Aunt Henrietta looked after Lottie for the first 11 years of her life. After that, she was raised with the Thomson children in Leith. Tom already had two mothers (with his Aunt Henrietta) but Lottie was his third little mother.

Life went relatively well for the Thomsons until 1883. The death of Tom's infant[xv] brother James that year shook them up. Five-year-old Tom was trundled off to the Leith church for the funeral along with the other siblings—no doubt marching down the dusty summer road to the nearby Leith Presbyterian Church. The customs of village grieving would have imprinted on young Tom during the formal mourning: neighbours' visits to the parlour, the fussing of church ladies, Sunday clothing, serious handshakes, and food and drink at the wake—lots of it.

The next significant occasion was happier. Lottie Tripp married James Gilchrist of

Right: *Leith, Ontario*, photo, TFC.

Left: *Elizabeth Thomson Harkness,* photo, TFC.

Note that this photo was taken in Chatham, Ontario where Elizabeth was said to have studied.

Sullivan on January 16, 1889; her 'sister' Elizabeth was her witness. Although Tom would have attended community weddings before then, for this very first family nuptial the Thomsons pulled out all the stops. Tom was 12-years-of-age when the singing and dancing of neighbours rang out into the winter night. You may be sure that young Tom had a dance with the bride as all his life Tom was fond of dancing. At various points during the celebrations at Rose Hill Farm, the Thomson children played the musical instruments their father purchased from a T. Eaton Co. catalogue. Tom played the cornet he had for the Leith Brass Band (and later orchestra) and switched at will to the mandolin, the instrument he loved his whole life. Tom's sister Minnie told biographer Blodwen Davies that, "They played rather intoxicating dance music and with a flawless maple floor in the hall, a good time was a foregone conclusion."[xvi]

Top: *The Gilchrist Children* August 6, 1899, photo, from left Margaret Thomson age 1; May Catherine age 5; James Hunter age 9 years. PF358S1F1I21 GRM.

Bottom: *George Thomson* photo, TFC.

The Gilchrists had seven children over the course of their marriage. Tom knew the four born in the Sullivan area: James, 1890; Russell, 1892; May Catherine[xvii], 1894 and Margaret, 1898. Tom was much affected by the death of little Russell in 1894. He was 17-years-old when his nephew died. The funeral reminded him of the death of his own wee brother James. Tom was at loose ends at that time in 1894. His sister Minnie reported that he became very restless and discontented. He'd left off his schooling and his mother had denied his wish to sail the Great Lakes. The death was one more weight. The woods and hills became an escape and a solace.

Tom didn't see much of Lottie and her family after the Gilchrists moved first to Keewatin and then later to Winnipeg but his love of children sprang, in large part, from the niece and nephews born to Lottie when he was 13, 15 and 17-years-old. Lottie kept in touch with the family through her letters and when Tom died, her 'father' John and 'sister' Elizabeth each gave her works[1] painted by her 'brother' Tom.

———

The departure of his eldest brother George in 1889 affected Tom deeply. George gained 'freedom' from the farm and its chores when he came into his inheritance from grandfather Tam; Tom, at 12-years-of-age had another nine years to go before he would be 'free'. George went first to the Canadian Business College in Chatham to study and from there to Seattle where he opened a business school. He married, had a son, studied to be a lawyer and then

[1]John Thomson gave Lottie *Stormy Weather,* watercolour, 1908, *Snow in the City,* oil 1913–1914 and Elizabeth gave Lottie *Spring, Algonquin,* oil, 1914. In addition she received *Northern Clouds,* Fall 1913, oil, from the estate.

15

tossed it all in for art in 1906, after his wife, Euphemia McLaren Thomson, died. George's son, known as George-the-Second or George M. (for McLaren), visited Owen Sound most summers and became well acquainted with his Leith family and its neighbours.[1]

George Sr. remarried in Owen Sound on April 16, 1914. Tom attended his oldest brother's wedding to Jean Telford—held at the Colonel Telford residence on East Eighth Street. "The entire house was beautifully decorated with multi-colored sweet peas, white, rose and claret colored ones being combined effectively with ferns and palms. Above the bridal party were draped the Union Jack and Stars and Stripes, the gifts of two friends."[2] Tom knew Jean as she was the daughter of their father's old fishing pal Colonel James Pattison Telford—a neighbour from Leith days. Since George and Jean were both over 40 at the time of this wedding, and George was proper to the point of being stiff, the reception for the teetotaler brother was 'conservative'. The newlyweds left for New Haven, Connecticut after the wedding. George kept up with his painting and when he and Tom were home together, they talked art.

George was home from the U.S. on a visit when Tom went missing at Canoe Lake in 1917. He ended up

representing his family during the weeks of trauma that followed.

Tom's oldest biological sister, Elizabeth, received a lesser inheritance. Tam's will stipulated $500 less for each granddaughter as young women of the time were expected to have husbands provide. She married Thomas James Harkness (T.J.) from nearby Annan. Tom was at Elizabeth's wedding on January 14, 1892.

Jessie Harkness-Fisk at SS #17 Crosshill School, 1916, photo, Jessie Harkness Collection #89-3-23 O, wellesleyhistory.org.

Elizabeth and T.J. had three children with whom Tom was close: Norman, 1894; Jessie, 1895; and Thomas, 1899. Tom wrote to Elizabeth in 1904,

"… when you write, put in some news of how the bairns are and some of the happenings around Annan …"[xviii]

---

[1] *George-the-Second's maternal grandparents moved to 2722 E. 54th Street Owen Sound where F.R. McLaren was chief clerk in the treasurer's office from 1908–1932.*

[2] *"Thompson [sic] – Telford" newspaper article, undated, GRM vertical files.*

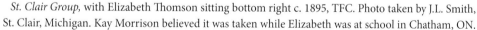

St. Clair Group, with Elizabeth Thomson sitting bottom right c. 1895, TFC. Photo taken by J.L. Smith, St. Clair, Michigan. Kay Morrison believed it was taken while Elizabeth was at school in Chatham, ON.

Annie Ainslie, photo, David Ainslie Collection, Comber, ON.

Tom first held babies Norm and Jessie when he was 17 and 18-years-old. When he was in Toronto, it was these bairns, and Lottie's, who drew him home. In her reminiscences about Tom, his sister Minnie wrote,

> *"He was never so happy as when amusing the children."* [xix]

When she was old enough, Tom's niece, Jessie Harkness, visited him in Toronto. She went on to be a teacher at S.S. #17 Crosshill[xx] in Wellesley Township during WWI. Tom may have visited his favourite niece in Wellesley, as he certainly wasn't afraid to ride the rails anywhere they went.

A case in point occurred when Elizabeth and T.J.'s son Norman Harkness[xxi] married Gladys Maud Ainslie in the little town of Comber, south of Lake St. Clair, on December 21, 1916. A large family contingent, including Tom, took the train through winter, wind-swept fields to be there.

The bridegroom may have met his bride as part of his travels as a salesman for Keystone View stereopticon, 3-D educational slides, but a more likely scenario emerged recently from photos held by two separate families. Helen Young,[xxii] a niece of the groom Norman Harkness, has a photo that shows her grandmother as a young Elizabeth Thomson in the St. Clair area in the 1890s. Elizabeth is seen with a group of professional-looking men and women—probably a class at the Chatham Business School.[1]

Norman's son, Ralph Harkness wrote in a letter in 2008, "None of the (Thomson) children ended up farming as a vocation. Each attended the Chatham Business School. These schools had sprung up to teach farm kids skills they could use in the move to the cities. So, over the course of time, each of John Thomson's kinder spent a year in Chatham—boarding with townspeople there."[xxiii]

Gladys Ainslie's descendant, David Ainslie[xxiv], has a photo in his family which shows Annie Ainslie, the bride's aunt. Side by side, the Helen Young and David Ainslie photos yield a surprise. Annie is in the group photo with Elizabeth! The photos connect the Thomsons of Leith with the Ainslies of Comber well before the turn of the century. How did that come about?

R.O.Y. Ainslie, Comber Ad; *R.O.Y. Ainslie Store,* Comber and *Train in Comber Station f*rom Comber and District Historical Society Facebook page with thanks to *Mark McKinlay and David Ainslie.*

[1] *The Chatham Business School was officially called the Canadian Business College.*

Research showed that 11 years before Confederation, when such deeds were possible, well-to-do Ainslie cousins Adam and George bought the whole town plot of Leith, all 460 acres of it. A year later in 1857, George Ainslie sold his share and headed to the Comber area in the western end of the province. Cousin Adam remained in Leith where among other endeavours, he built up "Ainslie's Wharf" from which Tom Thomson dove and fished. Gladys Ainslie, the bride in 1916, was the granddaughter of George Ainslie of Comber. Whatever had brought Elizabeth and Annie together in the 1890s, led in some way to the Cupid's shaft that brought these two communities together again.

In the winter of 1916, Tom, and his sister Elizabeth's family, took the Canadian Southern Railway (CASO) to Comber. That railway ran lumber, agricultural products and passengers between the Niagara frontier and Windsor at a time when the railroads and Great Lakes were major transportation routes. Comber Station was a CASO stop; the railroad hotel was a short walk away.

Just how much fun Tom had during his stay in Comber is open to speculation. Over a period of time the large Ainslie family had made itself rich in the lumber trade. They used their wealth to buy up the local hotels and then they dried them up. The three story brick Grand Central Hotel near the railroad station had 20 bedrooms but served only tea in the parlour. Perhaps, Ralph Oliphant Young (ROY) Ainslie, the father-of-the-bride, had libations for the festivities. ROY ran the local grocery store and might have had liquor suppliers. Even if he didn't,

Comber stories, passed down for generations, speculate that Tom Thomson made his own fun during his stay in Comber.

Tom found a female friend. David Ainslie heard that story about Tom's 'fun' from his grandmother Marcia Nichols Ainslie, a no-nonsense nurse. Marcia had married into the Ainslie family just a few years before the 1916 wedding. Marcia's unmarried sister, Emma Nichols, was in town for the holidays; it was natural for Marcia to take Emma to her niece's nuptials.

In David Ainslie's version of his grandmother's story, Tom Thomson was much taken by beautiful, petite Emma. He asked to sketch her and he did so—twice. When

Marcia found out about Emma's private sittings, she chided her for allowing such 'attentions'. The story is unclear as to whether Emma or Marcia ripped up the Thomson sketches, but they are gone. Emma Nichols later married a Methodist minister. Tom left for his last spring in Algonquin Park.

The story of Tom Thomson in Comber, Ontario, places him into a new area of the province and connects Leith and Comber. It shows that

even in 1916 when Tom was engrossed with Toronto artist friends, he made time to share family milestones.

And, contrary to the story of 'one true love' in the final years of Tom's life, the Emma Nichols incident demonstrates that Tom enjoyed the company of many beauties in life's great dance.

Tom's brother Henry came into his inheritance in 1893 and used it to head west through Chatham to Seattle. In 1897 he lived with his brother George and six-year-old George-the-Second at George's in-laws, the McLarens.[xxv] Henry studied at the business college that George and McLaren founded and then worked in a variety of different fields. In 1900 he married Letty Maude James[xxvi] of Olympia, Washington. Their son Fraser James Thomson was born June 16, 1901. Tom might have made it to Seattle in time for Henry's marriage, but, no matter if he missed that event. He had two nephews in Seattle with the birth of little Fraser.

Tom enjoyed young George and Fraser for the next four years—more bairns to amuse!

Ralph followed the family route to Seattle when he came into his inheritance in 1901. He boarded with Mabel and Pitt Shaw, as did Tom at that time. Ralph fell in love with the Shaw's daughter, Ruth. Tom and Ralph probably had a few discussions about the 'young' beauties of the boarding house as both Ruth and Alice Lambert, a part time boarder, were significantly younger than the men around the piano at the boarding house. Tom was 11 years older than Alice and Ralph was 10 years older than Ruth. Perhaps, Ruth and Alice had moments of giggly girl talk about the tall and handsome Thomson brothers. Tom was long gone, however, when Ralph married 18-year-old Ruth on December 25, 1906. Ralph's witnesses in King, Seattle, were his brother Henry and his sister-in-law Letty. Henry and Ralph ended up as fruit farmers in the Tacoma area. Tom had few interactions with his brothers Ralph and Henry after he left Seattle.

Tom's sisters Minnie and Louisa left Owen Sound in 1908 after they married the farming Henry brothers, William and James of Leith. Louisa and James Henry married first on February 28, 1907.[xxvii] George came home from the U.S. for the wedding to be his sister's witness. Minnie was Louisa's other witness. Tom was on hand from Toronto for partying, sketching and seasonal game.

Actually Tom spent a great deal of time in Owen Sound in 1907. There was Louisa's wedding in February; the many sketches in his leather-bound sketch book[xxviii] attest to summer visits. Then there was another wedding in the winter. Minnie and William Henry tied the knot on December 27 that same year. There were once again boisterous festivities in the Thomson home in Owen Sound.

Tom, who had become more confident with oils, presented Minnie with a painting as a joint Christmas and wedding gift. Early in the spring of 1908, the quartet of Minnie, Louisa, William and James Henry headed west to farm on the prairies. They moved a few times but always moved together. They had one child among them—Gibson Henry, born to Minnie and William in December 1912. Tom may have seen this nephew once in Owen Sound when Minnie visited in 1915. Tom did see his brothers-in-law in 1912 when they escorted the body of their mother Janet Gibson Henry home from the west for burial in the Leith cemetery.

Tom did not make it west for the 1917 wedding of his nephew George-the-Second. Young George had fallen in love with Lillias M. Henry while spending time in Pense, Saskatchewan with his uncles and aunts. Lillias was almost 20 years younger than her brothers James and William Henry but two years older than her bridegroom. Nothing describes the strong connections in the Thomson family better than the life of George-the-Second. He was born in Seattle where he was surrounded by Thomson uncles, including of course, Tom; he spent summers in Leith with his Thomson relatives; he met his bride among Thomson relatives out west and he married among uncles and aunts.

Tom's youngest sister, Margaret (Peggie), left home in 1905 when her inheritance came in. She went to Ottawa to train as a teacher and then worked in Timmins. Tom visited with Peggie while she was in teacher training. Art historian Joan Murray's remarks on *Decorative Landscape, Quotation from Henry van Dyke* show that Tom worked on his art and lettering during the visit: "Mary E. McIntire was rooming in the same boarding house as Thomson in Ottawa. She saved this work from the garbage where Thomson had thrown it because he had made the mistake of not leaving a space between the two words 'despise nothing'."[xxix]

Peggie's kindergarten sample book in the National Archives contains a pastel drawing purported to be by Tom. Tom's favourite niece, Jessie Harkness, recalled that he often helped his sister Peggie with her art samples for school.[xxx]

Tom kept up with his sister's news. He commented in a 1917 letter to his father, "I hope that Peggie didn't start away too soon after her sickness and that she will be all right at North Bay."[xxxi] In 1916, Margaret's future husband, William Muir Twaddle lived in North Bay. Peggie had gone there when young William enlisted and was in basic training. He sailed with the 159th Battalion, the Algonquins[xxxii], in November 1916.

In 1920 when Peggie was 36-years-old, she married William (who later changed his name to Tweedale). He was 26-years-of age. They settled in the High Park area of Toronto.

Tom was seven-years-old when Peggie was born. He watched her grow and took great pleasure in her. Peggie was 14-years-old when Tom left with his inheritance. During the years Tom was away, Peggie grew into a lovely young lady. Tom encouraged her teaching career. Peggie, in her turn, championed Tom all her life. She died in Toronto in 1979—the last living representative of the Thomson siblings.

Fraser, the youngest Thomson sibling, went east to Outremont, now part of Montreal, when he inherited his share of his grandfather's money. The handsome young man was a haberdasher by training. Fraser visited with Tom in Toronto in 1910 and they shared a visit to an art exhibition.

Art Gallery – Toronto Exhibition c. 1910, Postcard, Mary Cook, PD.

Fraser was living in Saskatoon, near his sisters Minnie and Louisa, when on October 6, 1915 he went back to Owen Sound to marry socialite, Ina Elspeth Legate. Ina's father William Legate had constructed the Legate Building at 790 2nd Ave. E. in Owen Sound in 1906. In 1914 the Legates opened the Owen Sound Furniture House in the building. The Legates clearly had the wherewithal to throw a huge wedding feast. Could Tom resist attending this wedding?

In addition to weddings, there were holidays and Thomson birthdays to celebrate. Tom would have made a Thanksgiving or two in the 34 years before he discovered his love of Algonquin Park. A relative remembers "Auntie", meaning Henrietta, bringing the ducks to the table along with vegetables and potatoes.

Tom's many interactions with family don't feature prominently in the art historical narrative yet like an undercoat of paint, they occasionally shine through. Biographer Blodwen Davies recounted an incident when Tom and his eldest brother were home in Owen Sound for a family visit at the same time, probably in the summer of 1907. Tom was disturbed by George's comments on one of his works. "At two o'clock he got up and dressed and slipped out of the house. By breakfast time he was back with a sketch that an-

swered his brother's criticism."[xxxiii] In another incident Davies describes how Fraser quizzed Tom as to why he didn't like a particular piece in an exhibition. Tom had replied that the artist had to paint as he saw the scene if it was going to be natural and last. According to Tom, there had been too much artifice in the work. These incidents indicate that Tom cared not only about his family, but also about what his family thought about art.

These glimpses of Tom are very different from those of the iconic lone canoeist paddling towards the horizon. We see a teenage Tom standing at the Leith grave site of a young babe, a young man dancing with his sisters at their weddings, Tom riding a train through winter fields to a nephew's wedding in Comber; he's talking art with his brother George, playing with his nephews in Seattle, taking his brother Fraser to an art exhibition in Toronto, visiting his sister Peggie in Ottawa and talking about young women with his brother Ralph in their shared boarding house room. One could say,

"Tommy, we hardly knew ye!"

Top Left: *Floradora Girl,* programme cover, Broadway musical, 1900, PD.

Top Right: *Floradora Poster,* PD.

Bottom: *Canadian Business College, Chatham, 1910,* TRL-VR.

Next Page: *Gold! Gold! Gold! Gold!,*
published in the *Seattle Post Intelligencer,* July 17, 1897.

CHAPTER FOUR

From Farm to City Life – 1898-1904

Tom Thomson's life underwent significant changes at the turn of the 20th century. He left small town farm life and started an apprenticeship as a machinist at Owen Sound's Wm. Kennedy & Sons—which he left after eight months. Then he completed a study period at the Canadian Business College in Chatham. He also generally cut loose with friends and fun. Tom's Leith pal Allan Ross said, "I don't think Tom's stay in Chatham did him much good. He seemed to me at the time to be drifting."[xxxiv] Well, Tom was young and, at 21-years-of age, he was finally free to do as he liked.

After eight fun-filled months in Chatham, Tom joined his brothers George and Henry who'd preceded him to Seattle, Washington State. Over the next two years, their brother Ralph also joined them[xxxv], as did many friends from Leith, including Horace Rutherford and his future brother-in-law William Henry. 'Go west young man' was clearly a strong theme at the turn of the century.

Young men sought opportunities in the robust new endeavours that developed after the *Seattle Post Intelligencer* on July 17,1897 screamed, "GOLD! GOLD! GOLD! GOLD!"

GOLD! GOLD! GOLD! GOLD!

Sixty-Eight Rich Men on the Steamer Portland.

STACKS OF YELLOW METAL!

Some Have $5,000, Many Have More, and a Few Bring Out $100,000 Each.

THE STEAMER CARRIES $700,000.

Special Tug Chartered by the Post-Intelligencer to Get the News.

Top Left: *Girl's Head,* c. 1908, Tom Thomson, oil, Private Collection.

Lower Left: *Seattle Engraving Company,* photo. Tom Thomson in red vest, Ralph Thomson second from the right. Others unknown. Henry Thomson worked as a bookkeeper in a stationary store and George for Acme Business College, the company he created. Image courtesy of John A. Libby Fine Art.

Right: *T*om Thomson (Canadian 1877–1917) *Study of a Woman's Head around 1904,* ink and coloured pencil over graphite on paper, 10.8 x 8.1 cm. Collection of the Tom Thomson Art Gallery, Owen Sound, gift of Fraser Thomson, brother of Tom Thomson, 1967, Photo credit: Michelle Wilson.

Historians estimate the Klondike Gold Rush drew over 70,000 people into the area—and not just as prospectors but also to support the Gold Rush economy. There were enough Grey County boys in Seattle to warrant a newspaper photo—a clipping of which their neighbour's descendant, Jaffray Rutherford, had in his possession in 2011.[xxxvi]

Alice Elinor Lambert (1886–1981), Public Member Photos, Ancestry.ca.

Tom first studied at a Seattle business school founded by his brother George,[xxxvii] and then started a series of jobs from elevator boy to graphic artist. He boarded with Mabel and Pitt Shaw even when they moved from one house to another. At the time, rooming or boarding houses were common domiciles for people of all ages. They provided affordable rooms, shared bathrooms and half or full board.

Many evenings Mrs. Shaw played the piano in the parlour[xxxviii] and the boarders held concerts. Ralph and Tom's musical friends frequently enlarged the ensemble. According to letters in the possession of art historian Joan Murray, boarder Alice Elinor Lambert remembered Tom singing *In the Shade of the Sheltering Palm,*[xxxix] a song from a musical called *Floradora.* "He would stand there tall and dark and slender, singing in his clear tenor, and the other boarders, the family and I would sit around and beg him to sing."[xl] Tom's brother Ralph noted that Tom played the violin or mandolin almost daily and that they frequently attended music events at local theatres.

Ralph Thomson had two years in Seattle to observe Tom's nascent endeavours as an artist. According to Ralph, Tom drew in his room, went sketching and often worked all night trying different design and advertising ideas with pen and ink, water colour and black and white wash. One work from this time, *Study of a Woman's Head c. 1903,* looks like a Floradora girl. The demure, fully clothed sextette of beauties from the musical *Floradora* was an international sensation.

27

Each dancer was 'the ideal woman' at 5' 4" and 130 pounds (162 cm and 58.9 kg). Their silhouettes, considered lithe at the time, became a staple in American musical theatre. Tom knew the musical as he sang a song from it. His sketch may have been his attempts at a Floradora girl.

At the same time, Tom also experimented with oil paints.[xli] A work showing Puget Sound,[xlii] a complex waterway of channels, inlets, estuaries and islands, is displayed on the *West Wind* website; it's one of Tom's earliest attempts at oils.[xliii] Ralph found that it was usually 'curtains' for fishing whenever an interesting scene caught Tom's interest. He'd set down his fishing rod and out would come his sketch pad and pencils. Occasionally he'd try to paint that special scene later.

In 1904 Tom abruptly left this convivial life in Seattle. His decamping had to do with the Shaw's occasional boarder, Alice Elinor Lambert. One story has 18-year-old Alice giggle during Tom's marriage proposal; another account has Tom divert his friend Horace

Rutherford back to Owen Sound as Horace had made his own 'proposal' to Alice. In this version Tom considered Horace unsuitable for Alice and acted swiftly to save her. Whatever happened, Tom abruptly left Seattle in 1904—with Horace Rutherford in tow.

George, Ralph and Henry Thomson remained in the U.S. and married American women.

Canadian art history probably has Alice Elinor Lambert to thank that Tom Thomson did not settle permanently in the United States.

Seattle Snapshot

While in Seattle, Tom worked for both Maring & Blake (Maring & Ladd in Tom's time), Engravers and Seattle Engraving Co.

Left: *Maring & Blake Engravers* Ad, Seattle Directory, PD.

Centre: *Seattle Engraving Co.* Ad, Seattle Directory, PD.

Top Right: *Horace and his father David Rutherford*, photo, Rutherford Family Collection, thanks to Twila Rutherford.

Lower Right: *ACME Business School,* Ad, Seattle Directory, PD. George Thomson's and F.R. McLaren's School is on the second floor, right, above the Seattle Art Company.

Top Left: *John Thomson and Colonel James Pattison Telford,*
photo, TFC.

Right: *Thomson family home, 528 Fourth Avenue East,
Owen Sound,* photo, TFC.

Lower Left: *Legg Brothers Photoengraving, Jordan Street,*
courtesy of Nancy Lang.

CHAPTER FIVE

New Life in Toronto and Many New Friends

"How are you feeling? Did you have good fishing out at Jackson's this summer? I have to thank you people for the good time I had while in Huntsville and hope that sometime we may have a fishing trip where the fish bite." Tom Thomson letter to John McRuer, October 17, 1912

Tom Thomson had serious setbacks behind him by the time he was 27-years-old. He returned to his parents to regroup, but, like him, John and Margaret Thomson were in a period of transition. When none of five sons proved willing to carry on with agriculture, they sold Rose Hill Farm. They lived for a short time with their daughter Elizabeth Harkness in Annan before moving to 8th Street in Owen Sound, near John Thomson's fishing crony, Colonel James Pattison Telford whose brother William at that time was a Member of Parliament for North Gray.[xliv]

Tom's reinvention of himself was accomplished on his own. He started by buying a new leather-covered sketchbook; he took trips south to scout out a future in Toronto. Tom had good credentials from the graphic art firms[xlv] in Seattle, and with them, he secured a position as a senior artist with Legg Brothers Photoengraving on Jordan Street. The job was to start in June 1905.

The question of lodgings was settled when he met up with Harry Watson, a buddy from Chatham days. Harry's parents, Joseph and Sara[xlvi] Watson, had moved from Chatham to 54 Elm Street in Toronto; they took in boarders. Their rooms held a medical student and a smattering of devout Methodists. The latter were fitting tenants as both Sara Thursa Watson and Joseph Robert Watson were the offspring of Methodist preachers. Their particular branch of the faith, called Primitive Methodism, was evangelical and noisy. They believed in open-air camp meetings and mass conversions.

Sara was the daughter of the Reverend Abraham Heyhurst who preached in Paris, Bonsanquet and Chatham. Joseph was the son of Reverend George Humphrey Watson who served ministries in Plympton Township and in Brant County, before Markdale in Grey County. These reverends moved their families around in what amounts to a great geographic exercise for small town Ontario at the time of Confederation. Revival events brought the Watsons and Heyhursts into contact. Their children understood the life and found one another.

Tom settled in and lived with the demonstrably religious Watsons for nearly four years, and yet art history has never placed Tom Thomson in a den of revivalists.[xlvii] It's an odd image for Tom but not for 'Toronto the good', which in 1905 was a bastion of morals and Methodism. Tom's own street was home to the Elm Street Methodist Church. The Watsons' prayerful boarding house was a significant change from the lighthearted, music-making times at the Shaws in Seattle.

Tom visited his only relative in Toronto in the months before work started. "Uncle" William Brodie was a cousin to his long-deceased grandmother, Elizabeth

Brodie Thomson.[xlviii] Tom's parents, John and Margaret, had visited the old gentleman when Tom was a boy—a habit from John's own youth. Uncle Brodie, was a dentist by profession but a naturalist by passion. He was going strong in spite of health problems with his eyes.[xlix]

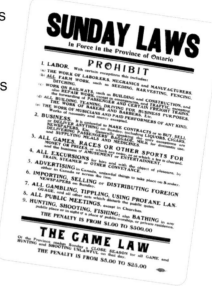

The 72-year-old Dr. Brodie took a new lease on life just a few years before in 1903 when the Ontario government purchased his large specimen collection which featured plant galls (abnormal outgrowths of plant tissues caused by parasites invading the plant). The government hired him to work on readying his specimens for what would be the province's first museum for biological collections. Brodie found this task enlivening as he was finally able to leave dentistry behind. And, although Brodie didn't live to see his collection installed in the museum, Tom might have. The Royal Ontario Museum opened to the public in March of 1914.

Left: *Sunday Laws in force in the province of Ontario,* ephemera, PD.

Above: *ROM, 1914,* photo from "New Royal Ontario Museum, Bloor Street West, Formally Opened by the Duke of Connaught", the *News,* March 19, 1914, PD.

Back in 1905, however, the lively Brodie continued to spark intellectual activity for family and friends. The people in Brodie's circle included Ernest Thompson Seton, a.k.a. Black Wolf, naturalist and co-founder of the Boy Scout movement, and Augustus Vogt, founder of the Toronto Mendelssohn Choir.

In his youth, Tom had exposure to such stellar visitors to Uncle Brodie's home. He might even have been one of the boy guests Brodie roused by placing a garter snake in his bedclothes—a prank described in Louise Hertzberg's book about Brodie, *A Pocketful of Galls*. Tom certainly accompanied Brodie on legendary, long Sunday walks in the Don River Valley. Art historian, Joan Murray, describes Brodie as someone who fine-tuned Thomson to look intensely at nature's offerings.

All the food Tom ate in the Brodie home was organic—not surprising for a time when Canada was young. William and Jane Brodie grew their own vegetables and herbs. Convicts at the nearby Don Jail tended and milked the Brodies' cows as part of their duties at the jail's farm in the area of Toronto called Riverdale. One would have expected nothing less 'natural' from parents who named six daughters after flowers: Jessamine, Lillie, Daisy, Rose, Violet and Verbena. Their only son was William, as in the plant Sweet William, of course. Sadly, young 'Willie', as he was known, drowned in the Assiniboine River in 1883 when he was on a specimen-gathering expedition organized by family friend, Ernest Thompson Seton.

Dr. Brodie never totally recovered from his son's drowning at 23-years-of-age, but he did channel his loss. He mentored young naturalists for the rest of his life. Hertzberg says, "Brodie had great sympathy for and understanding of young men."[1] Tom Thomson was one of the young men Brodie took under wing.

Uncle William Brodie

Opposite Page: *Dr. William Brodie*, Owen Staples, oil, University of Toronto Art Collection, Faculty of Dentistry.

Left: *Tom Thomson Man with a Mustache, profile*, c. 1905 graphite on wove paper, 20.9 x 12.5 cm Gift of Leanora D. McCarney, Hull, Quebec, 1990 National Gallery of Canada, Ottawa Photo.

Right: *Ernest Thompson Seton,* George Grantham Bain collection at the Library of Congress.

Ernest Thompson Seton

Tom's life in Toronto started well, but, it was not all healthy food, invigorating conversation and long walks in ravines. Tom took measure of his new circumstances and found things wanting. He wrote to his sister Louisa[li] that the Primitive Methodists in his boarding house were too loud in their devotions. Two slightly different stories, one in a letter by Louisa and another by sportswriter Trent Frayne in *Macleans Magazine* in 1953, tell of Tom knocking on their door to ask the clamouring worshippers to be less zealous. Both tales have Tom assert that they didn't need to raise their voices to such a great extent, as the Almighty couldn't possibly be **that** far away. One can almost see what Tom's pal Allan Ross described: "He (Tom) had a sort of funny little silent laugh and as his sense of humor was a pretty active one, one often heard, or rather saw it."[lii]

In the same article, Frayne said that whenever Tom went downstairs from his third floor room to sit in the living room to await the evening meal, he sat in silence. His sister Louisa explained that Tom's piety was quiet. "His religion went deeper than most people knew and could be summed up in a few words … do justly, love mercy, walk humbly, and say nothing about it."

Tom had a few further complaints. He told his Legg Brothers co-worker Stuart Logan Thompson that he was tired of the food at his place up Yonge Street. He was especially worn down by the repeat appearances of Barney's chop suey. Since Barney wasn't listed as a boarder at 54 Elm Street in the *Toronto City Directory*, this Barney might have been the Watsons' cook using up leftovers.

Tom had his complaints, but he enjoyed the renewed friendship with the Watson's son Harry. Harry Watson had apprenticed as a painter earlier in Chatham when he and Tom were friends there, but in 1905, he worked with his father at the Watson Harness Company at 718 Yonge Street. Horse drawn transportation at that time was in transition to automobiles but the Watson establishment was rising to the occasion. They sold leather suitcases, trunks and valises in addition to harnesses.

Harry Watson lived near his parents with Charlotte May Kitchen and baby Wilfrid born in October 1904. Tom first met Harry's beloved "Lottie" in December 1905 and from then on he spent time with them. On February 6, 1907, when Harry Watson married Lottie, Tom presented them with a watercolour he'd painted of her from a photograph. In Joan Murray's *Catalogue Raisonné* this work is listed but its whereabouts is unknown.

Top: *Faculty of Medicine Building, King's College Circle,*
postcard chuckmantorontonostalgia.wordpress.com.

Lower: *Faculty of Medicine, University of Toronto, Graduating Class 1907.*
University of Toronto Living History page.
Dr. McRuer is on the far left, fifth row from top.

The irksome Primitive Methodists of Elm Street aside, Tom did develop a good relationship with one boarder, John McRuer, a third year medical student. They were quickly friends and remained close for almost a decade.

Tom was seven years older than John McRuer, but, other than that, the two were similar. They were of Scottish Presbyterian stock and from farms near small communities. They loved to fish and hunt; they read voraciously and they attended music events. When they were young, both travelled long distances to libraries that were former Mechanics' Institutes; Tom's library was in Owen Sound and John's in Ayr, where it was on the ground floor of the Masonic Lodge.[liii] Both men were intensely interested in the natural world, and spent large amounts of quiet time outdoors. John and Tom were also both passionate about Ontario's wild north.

John McRuer came to Toronto in 1903 to study at the brand new Faculty of Medicine building on King's College Circle. He had classes in the new lecture theatre there and at other university faculties, including the Department of Biology where Dr. William Brodie might well have lectured. When John graduated in 1907, he planned to intern with Dr. Francis L. Howland in Huntsville.

ANGIE LITTLEFIELD

Watson Harness Company at 718 Yonge Street, Ancestry.ca.

Main Street Brampton, postcard, 1910, TPL-SC, PD.

Howland had helped set up a subscription hospital that was well equipped and a forerunner to Medicare in Canada. The hospital allowed subscribers to purchase medical protection to cover the cost of future treatment. S. Bernard Shaw describes Howland's service for lumbermen in "Medicare in Algonquin Park".[liv] For Dr. John McRuer, Huntsville was a progressive choice.

Between 1905 and 1907 Tom and John shared meals at their Elm Street boarding house. They also shared stories of lectures, labs, graphic and visual arts, concerts, books, visits home and for Tom, tales about sketching trips. Tom regularly went sketching on the Humber and Don Rivers with Legg Brothers co-workers. Among his works from this time is an ink drawing of the Don River. According to Joan Murray, Tom gave this ink drawing to Samuel Albert Hutchinson,[lv] (Hutcheson) a Huntsville lawyer with whom Tom hunted. Hutcheson was a son of the *Forester* newspaper proprietor George Hutcheson and a Masonic Lodge brother of John McRuer.

Tom also pencilled a portrait of a man with a mustache around this time. The man looks very like Uncle Brodie's close friend, the naturalist Ernest Thompson Seton. Tom likely met Seton at one of Brodie's walks and talks but Seton also happened to be the uncle of Tom's work colleague Stuart Logan Thompson.[lvi] With these connections, Tom had twice the chance to meet Seton. Young Stuart Thompson was a birder and a specimen-gatherer like his Uncle Ernest and like Tom's Uncle Brodie. All these men vibrated at the same frequency.

Ernest Thompson Seton, photo from "Boy Scout trail: Organization can trace its roots back to Cos Cob and Ernest Thompson Seton", greenwichtime.com.

On top of good connections to Seton, Tom also had a two year window in which to draw him. The well-travelled naturalist's daughter Anna was born in Manhattan in 1904 and Seton, the intrepid traveller, rested a while. On short trips he visited family in Toronto and Brodie. By 1907, Seton was on a 2,000 mile (3,219 km) canoe odyssey across northern Canada with Edward Preble of the U.S. Biological Survey.

Tom probably seized an opportunity between 1905 and 1907 for a quick sketch of the famous man.

Seton's travels, naturalist studies, books and illustrations intrigued Canadians and Americans alike. Tom Thomson, an avid reader, would have read or known about *Wild Animals I Have Known* (1898), *Biography of a Grizzly* (1899) and *Animal Heroes* (1905)—all successful books.

There is more evidence for this speculation about the drawing of the man with the mustache. From his youth, Tom was known to his siblings to be accurate in capturing likenesses. Tom's sister Minnie wrote to Blodwen Davies in 1931 saying that she could still, "see the whimsical grin when he got an extra good caricature." The likeness of the man with the mustache to Seton is remarkable.

Tom added a lively woman to this busy social life in Toronto. He did not let the Seattle experience with Alice Lambert put him off for very long. His new female companion, Elizabeth McCarnen, was the fourth of nine children born to Irish parents in Phelpston, Ontario, a small farming community located between Lake Simcoe and Georgian Bay. Elizabeth went to Toronto late in the 19th century to work as a domestic in the opulent Jarvis Street home of businessman and retired Ontario legislator Thomas Long.

Long had renovated 513 Jarvis Street in the Classical Revival Style, called it Woodlawn and lived there in luxury to his death in 1921.[lvii] Elizabeth's charm and fine sewing skills blossomed in these refined surroundings. She soon advanced to a position in the T. Eaton Company's prestigious Dressmaking Department—probably with a little help from the Longs. There was another change for Elizabeth when her oldest sister Maggie (Margaret) married bookkeeper John Jennings King in 1906. The newly married couple opened up rooms at 39 Pembroke Street. There they welcomed Maggie's siblings, including "Miss Elizabeth of the T. Eaton Company.[lviii]

Elizabeth McCarnen, photo, Paul Simon Collection.

It's not clear where Tom met Elizabeth but both loved to dance. Elizabeth's descendants[lix] attest to her lifelong love of dancing and it is well documented that Tom danced all through his youth. In a 1977 article in the *Owen Sound Sunday Times,* 74-year-old Wilson Buzza, who frequently visited Rose Hill Farm, recalled it as a great place to dance. He reported, "I can still see Tom Thomson dancing." The Thomson family held regular ceilidhs in their Rose Hill kitchen and parlour and even after Tom went to Toronto he returned to Owen Sound for dances in Leith and Annan. Tom and Elizabeth's six year age discrepancy, with Elizabeth the older, made no difference when the two went dancing, for walks in the Don

"Woodlawn, E.J. Lennox architect", photo, *Toronto Architectural Eighteen Club Second Annual Exhibition 1902,* at Ontario Society of Artists' Galleries, King St. W. p 103. Jarvis Collegiate sits on the site of Woodlawn.

Valley, to the Canadian National Exhibition and to art exhibitions.[lx] Tom Thomson and Elizabeth McCarnen were out and about and having fun.

A Thomson art work of a lady in her garden dates from this period. Joan Murray ascribes *Portrait of a Lady in her Garden* to being an image of a woman who boarded in the same house as Tom. Elizabeth McCarnen told her niece, Rita Tomlinson, that Tom briefly roomed at 39 Pembroke Street with the Kings and McCarnens in 1908—but more of that later.

Tom was busy with John McRuer in 1906 and 1907. John had fallen in love. Upon graduation in the spring of 1907 the new doctor interned as planned with Dr. Howland at the General Hospital in Huntsville. In 1901 this hospital was described as the best appointed in Northern Ontario: "… brick, four stories, 60x40 feet, (18x12m) sunbathed corridors, convalescent wards, smoking room, abundance of water from town waterworks …. Electric lights, speaking tubes, elevator, telephone and telegraph connections open night and day … excellently lighted operating room with all modern appliances for aseptic treatment."[lxi] The praise went on and on.

Dr. McRuer also managed to be on staff at Grace Hospital in Buffalo. Dr. McRuer likely met Edythe Norma Bullock in Buffalo. Although Edythe and her sister Evelyn were raised in Brampton, Ontario, in the 19th century, by the 20th century, things had changed for women. Edythe's older sister Evelyn lived in Buffalo with her father and worked as a telephone operator. We know that Tom went to New York State as Tom's co-worker Stuart Thompson recalled Tom's enthusiasm for Americans after that visit. Tom had loved a band concert he'd attended there.[lxii]

With John courting and interning in 1907, Tom spent a good portion of that summer in Owen Sound where he continued to fill his sketchbook. There were pencil sketches of his brother George[lxiii] on a summer visit home with his son, George-the-Second. Tom drew Aldersyde, the Harkness Farm of his sister Elizabeth's in-laws, the McKeen home of his Leith neighbours, Kemp's Mill Pond, and a portrait of his favourite niece—Jessie Harkness—who was then nearly 12-years-of-age. There were soon over 20 works in Tom's leather-bound sketch book.

Meanwhile, Dr. John McRuer had definitively decided on Huntsville for his first medical practice. The July 23, 1908, issue of the Huntsville *Forester* noted, "Dr. McRuer is well and favourably known to many in and around

Huntsville who will join in welcoming him; wishing him success in his ventures."[lxiv] On August 1, 1908, Dr. John McRuer opened his office on Main Street, right beside W.J. Rodman's store, where homemade ice cream, oysters and hot drinks were on the menu. The September 24, 1908, social news in the *Forester* announced the visit of John's father from Ayr. John McRuer Sr. had come to drop off a wagon, known as a driver, for his son's medical rounds in the country.

On February 16, 1909 when Edythe and John McRuer married, Tom Thomson was at their side as best man and witness.[lxv] The other witness was Edythe's sister Evelyn. The marriage and reception were held in the Bullock home in Brampton. After the honeymoon, the newlyweds headed to Huntsville to start John's medical practice.

While these dramatic changes took place in John's life, Tom relied on his friend to help him through his unsettling events. Tom had found the noisy Elm Street boarding house overwhelming after his friend left. He took up Elizabeth McCarnen's invitation to board at her sister Maggie's place on Pembroke Street. He enjoyed the company of the Kings and McCarnens and a return to music. He frequently played his mandolin there.[lxvi] He had no complaints about the cooking.

Elizabeth's reputation as a superb cook remains in the memories of her family after three generations. One story features Elizabeth McCarnen handing home-cooked morsels to Tom through a main floor window at the Elm Street boarding house.

Then life became complicated. In 1908 Elizabeth McCarnen's brother Bernard lost his wife, their sister Mary died and their mother was ill. Five young nephews and nieces were in need of care. Elizabeth's aging father and three brothers couldn't manage. Elizabeth was 37-years-old. If Elizabeth was contemplating matrimony, it was not a good time to leave Tom and Toronto. According to Elizabeth's descendants, Tom offered marriage but, it was not to be. Duty triumphed. Elizabeth McCarnen left for Phelpston.

Tom was adjusting to Elizabeth's departure when Uncle Brodie died. The meals and conversations of the lively Brodie home on Parliament Street passed into memory. Added to these losses was the destabilization of a change of job and residence. Tom left Legg Brothers for Grip Limited, very late in 1908 or early 1909. After Elizabeth was gone, Tom changed residence again. This time, he moved from the Kings' on Pembroke to Mrs. Esther Plewes' boarding house at 99 Gerrard Street.

Tom was glad to have his friend John McRuer and his own family for stability. Tom visited Owen Sound on weekends and went on excursions to the McRuers in Muskoka for painting, fishing, and hunting. When Tom arrived in Huntsville in the early summer of 1910, the young married couple were eager to tell him about an exciting episode. Dr. John McRuer had been front page news on June 9 when he treated a blood-soaked stabbing victim carried to his office after a nasty run-in with a jealous husband.

John and Edythe hosted John's brother, James McRuer at that time in 1910. He was in Huntsville to improve his health. Both brothers had respiratory ailments, but James' was more severe at that point. James had signed a contract to article with John's Masonic pal, Huntsville lawyer Samuel Albert Hutcheson, later that year. When the Hutcheson law practice proved quiet, James rode with his brother on his medical rounds in the country. Author Patrick Boyer in his article "McRuer in Muskoka" wrote, "gradually shaking off his illness, he (James McRuer) travelled with his brother to see patients in lonely country farms or cabins in the woods, a few times journeying all night along frozen moonlit lakes to handle emergencies."[lxvii]

Dominion Hotel, Huntsville, MHPC, 1986.75.271.

In later life, James McRuer described a scene in the Dominion Hotel where Tom stayed in 1910. Tom had been painting in the area, as he liked to do. He'd wandered as far as the borders of Algonquin Park. Back in his hotel room, he took fresh sketches out of his pack and excitedly spread out his preliminary boards for the brothers' viewing. When James showed interest, Tom allowed him to take any two he wanted. James selected *Pine Stump and Rocks* and *Sunset over Hills*. John McRuer took *A Northern Lake.* James described the air in the room as heady with the intoxicating aroma of oil paint.

43

From Left:

"Dr. John McRuer, Scotia Junction", Tom Thomson photo, *Bulletin 16, #34.*

"James McRuer, Scotia Junction", Tom Thomson photo, *Bulletin 16, #36.*

"William Smithson Broadhead, Scotia Junction", Tom Thomson photo, *Bulletin 16, #35.*

Tom visited the McRuers again in 1912 when he was en route to the Mississagi Forest Reserve with Grip Limited co-worker William Smithson Broadhead. Tom took separate photos of John and James McRuer, and of William Smithson Broadhead, at Scotia Junction where they'd gone for an outing.

Scotia Junction was a bustling railway hub and the Albion Hotel, seen in the background of Tom's photos, was an area attraction. It had a lovely dining room set around a potbellied stove. Although there are hints in art history that the group picnicked, it's interesting to speculate about a luncheon party of five at the Albion. The cocky, young Brit, William Smithson Broadhead probably weighed in on all subjects. Broadhead had lived in Toronto since 1910 and, based on his chatty letters home to Sheffield,[lxviii] he was never shy about sharing his opinions. With a doctor, lawyer, Edythe and two artists at the table, who knows where the conversation went. The *Titanic* had just sunk, the Chateau Laurier had opened in Ottawa, the first Calgary stampede was about to happen and Tom and John never ran out of fishing stories.

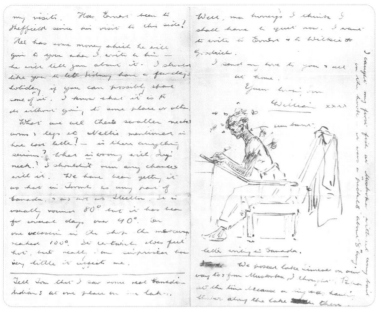

William Smithson Broadhead letter, July 5, 1910, captioned, "letter writing in Canada", SA, KD1980-15 p4.jpeg.

Albion Hotel, Scotia Junction, photo, MHPC 1969.492.6.

As well as possibly eating at the Albion Hotel, there were other area food locales to try. Huntsville hotels had catered to off-season lumbermen for decades, but by the time tourists and Tom hit the Muskokas, dining rooms were gentrified with fine tablecloths and expensive crystal. The Kent Hotel menu with its oysters and succotash showed typical offerings—great alternatives to boarding house food.

It was obvious on Tom's 1912 visit that John McRuer's health had deteriorated badly. He had full-blown tuberculosis, a common ailment in the early years of Canada. Dr. McRuer sold his Huntsville practice that winter and headed to Denver, Colorado, in pursuit of what he perceived to be better air. Tom never saw John again. The good doctor practiced medicine sporadically in the U.S., but unfortunately, on October 31, 1917, he died.

James McRuer went by train to Denver to bring back his brother's body for burial in the family plot at Ayr, not too long after George Thomson had arranged to bring his brother's body home from Canoe Lake to Leith.

In the year that Canada celebrated 50 years as a country, both Tom's and John's parents buried sons. Tom made it to 39-years-of-age, and his good friend John to 32. Their families, and Canada, lost a great deal of promise.

"We would have been very glad to have seen you again this summer, but hope you will stay much longer next season." John McRuer letter to Tom Thomson, November 1, 1912."

The Food Connection

The House of Industry, Elm Street, TRL-SC.

Tom's meals in Toronto from 1905 to1908 were mostly in his Elm Street boarding house where Sara Watson's cooking heritage influenced the fare. Sara's family, the Heyhursts, went back to the mill town of Rochdale in Lancashire, U.K. Her husband's family had British origins as well. They haled from Northampton, renowned for leather work. In 1642 the good men of Northampton made 4,000 shoes and 600 boots. No small wonder that a son of Northampton was a harness maker in Canada.

Mrs. Watson likely had the Elm Street cook serve up cost-effective British menus: corn beef hash with boiled cabbage, bangers and mash, fish and chips, and bubble and squeak—a great leftover disposer. Another factor that would have influenced menu planning at Elm Street was the location of the Watson boarding house.

City Hall from Elizabeth Street, 1924,
CTA, Fonds 1244, ft244_it0323a.

The Watson's place was in St. John's Ward, a notorious, densely populated slum bounded by Yonge Street and University Avenue at the east and west, and College and Queen Streets at the north and south. A Dickensian poor house, called the House of Industry, sat just down the street at 87 Elm Street. There, in return for work, the poorest of the poor received lodging, food and coal. Tom's grimy, dilapidated neighbourhood featured food stands locals set up to supplement their meagre incomes. Stale, toasted, white bread and tea were the regular fare for the poor. In Tom's four years at the Watsons, Chinese, Italian and Jewish immigrants crowded the streets where he lived and contributed to the food influences.

Since Tom specifically mentioned chop suey to co-worker Stuart Thompson, I searched for recipes expecting a Chinese source. Instead, on a trip to Huntsville to Muskoka Heritage Place, I found a recipe for chop suey in *Recipes from Muskoka.* Mrs. Ivan Knight had a chop suey recipe for leftover spaghetti.

Mrs. Ivan Knight's Chop Suey

Recipes from Muskoka, Huntsville, All Saints Anglican Church, 1951, page 40

"1 lb. hamburg, 2 tins tomato soup, ½ cup rice, 1 cup spaghetti, 2 small onions, fried in butter with meat

Method: Cook rice and spaghetti separately in boiling salted water until done. Mix all ingredients. Stir until heated through. Add salt and pepper to taste."

39 Pembroke Street, Toronto, photo Angie Littlefield. Tom lived there with the McCarnen/King Family after he left Elm Street and before he went to Gerrard Street. For some reason I picture him in the garret window. Nowadays, the house is a boarding house for Chinese immigrants.

Barney's chop suey might very well have meant variations on leftover pasta, as in the recipe above. The Ward contained many Italian immigrants. Then in the 1915 *The Toronto (Queen City of Canada) Cookbook,* I found a recipe that shows the thriving influence of Chinese immigrants in The Ward. Was this Barney's chop suey?

Chop Suey

"To make enough chop suey for five persons take one pound of fresh young pork and cut into small pieces, two chicken livers, two chicken gizzards and hearts, two stalks of celery and a half-ounce of ginger root. Put four tablespoons of olive oil in a saucepan and when hot add the meat, celery and ginger. As soon as fairly coloured, add one tablespoon vinegar, half-a-cup of boiling water, one teaspoon Worcestershire sauce, red and black pepper, cinnamon and cloves to taste. Simmer gently until the pork and giblets are nearly done; then add a small can of mushrooms and a half-cup of bean sprouts. If you cannot get the bean sprouts (They are abundant in Chinese groceries) you may use the quantity of French green peas, string beans chopped fine or asparagus tips. The bean sprouts must not cook too long, as they are better when not more than half done. Drain off the superfluous liquor, add a teaspoon of brown See Yu sauce (This also may be obtained in a Chinese grocery.) Serve with boiled rice."

I interviewed a descendant of Tom's girlfriend Elizabeth McCarnen, after I'd finished the research above. Imagine my surprise when great, grandnephew Paul Simon said that Elizabeth McCarnen told his grandmother that

Tom loved Chinese food.

Tom and Elizabeth often went to the Chinese Restaurant at the corner of Queen and Pembroke Streets. And there, the trail of Barney's chop suey finally grew cold.

Beyond chop suey, I found little else for the food connection for this chapter until I stumbled upon a 1903 menu for the Kent Hotel in Huntsville. I was intrigued by three types of oysters the menu offered as hors d'oeuvres. Rodman's, beside the McRuer's on Main Street, also served oysters. But since I had artist John Beatty making oyster stew at The Shack in a later chapter, I didn't need oysters just yet.

Instead, I tracked down the Kent Hotel's vegetable selection—succotash. I'd grown up with Sylvester, the cartoon cat as he cursed Tweety Bird. I didn't realize Sylvester's lisped expression, "Thufferin' Thuccotash", was based on a vegetable dish. The sweet corn and lima bean mixture called succotash derived from *Narragansett sohquttahhash,* or, broken-corn kernels. Recipes for the mixture were as inventive as the makers, but corn and beans of some sort always played a part.

I found Succotash in *Purity Flour Cookbook* by Miss E. Warner, Toronto and Winnipeg, Western Canada Flour Mills Co. Ltd., 1917, page 125

> "10 ears of corn, 1 quart Lima beans,
> 2 tablespoons butter, 1 teaspoon salt,
> ¼ teaspoon pepper, 1 cup sweet cream

> With a sharp knife cut the corn from the cobs and add to the Lima beans the last 15 minutes of cooking, when they are tender and water nearly all absorbed. This mixture should be cooked nearly dry. Add butter, seasonings and cream, and simmer for 10 minutes."

I pictured Tom, John and Edythe at a linen-clad table in the dining room of a gentrified Huntsville hotel. I watched in my imagination as they picked items from a leather-bound menu. A stiff waiter advanced to stand by their table, his nose snootily turned up to the tin ceiling tiles. Whatever they selected, it would have been a change of pace from boarding house chop suey and the food stalls in St. John's Ward where vendors swatted flies off their wares.

Dine like Tom Thomson. Make your selections from the Kent Hotel Menu.

Hotel Kent

Menu

OYSTERS

Blue Points   New York Counts   Extra Selects Stew

Consomme, Plain

SOUP   Consomme Vegetables

FISH

Boiled Georgian Bay Salmon   Anchovy Sauce

HORS D'OEUVERS

Celery   Radish   Olives

Lettuce   Green Onions

ROASTS

Prime Roast Sirloin of Beef   Browned Potatoes

Leg of Lamb, Mint Sauce

Roast Turkey, Cranberry Jelly   Roast Goose and Apple Sauce

ENTREE

Chicken Fricassee with Mushrooms   Macaroni a la Creme

GAME

Saddle Venison, Red Currant Jelly   Broiled Belgium Hare, Grape Jam

WINE

Golden Diana   Claret   Fine Old Port

VEGETABLES

Mashed Potatoes   A la Creme Potato   Hashed Brown Potatoes

Stewed Tomatoes   French Peas   Succotash

RELISHES

Gillards Relish   Crosse & Blackwells Walnuts   Heatons Chow-Chow

Mortons Mixed Pickles   Chili Sauce

Tomato Catsup   Worcestershire Sauce   Heinz Sweet Pickle

Harveys Sauce

SALADS

Lobster Salad   French Vegetable Salad

DESSERTS

English Plum Pudding, Brandy Sauce   Tapioca Cream Meringue

Lemon Pie   Apple Pie   Chocolate Cake

Fruit Cake   Cocoanut Cake

CHEESE

Roquefort   Young Canadian   McLarens Imperial

ICES

Pineapple   Orange   Strawberry Ice Cream

FRUIT, Etc

Oranges, Lion, Navel   Apples   Raisins, Connoisseur Clusters

Extra Selected Figs

English Walnuts   Filberts   Almonds

TEA AND COFFEE

Ceylon Tea   Green Tea   Mixed Tea   French Coffee

Crystal Ale   Cigars   Labatts Ale

Left: *Hotel Kent, 1898,* MHPC, 1970.813.

Right: *Hotel Kent Banquet Menu, Huntsville, 1902,* MHPC, 1986.75.265.2.

Interior of Albion Hotel, Scotia Junction, photo, MHPC 1969.284.3.

Top Left: *Tom Thomson at Canoe Lake*, photo, Sylvia (Hayhurst) Telford, Hayhurst Point. Tom Thomson, third from left, at Canoe Lake Station.

Lower Right: *Daydreaming (Portrait of Thoreau MacDonald)*, Tom Thomson, oil on panel 7.5x11.5 in. (19.1x29.2 cm), pencil sketch of a boy on the reverse and inscribed "Drawing and oil by Tom Thomson, looks about 1913–14, Thoreau MacDonald". Private collection. Reproduced with permission thanks to Katlin Rogers, Consignor Canadian Fine Art.

Lower Left: *Tom Thomson Cairn*, child placing flowers is Tom Baldwin, photo, Sylvia (Hayhurst) Telford.

CHAPTER SIX

J.E.H. and Thoreau MacDonald, for the Love of the Father and the Son

"He lived humbly but passionately with the wild. It made him brother to all untamed things of nature. It drew him apart and revealed itself wonderfully to him. It sent him out from the woods only to show these revelations through his art and it took him to himself at last." J.E.H.MacDonald inscription on the Tom Thomson Memorial Cairn at Canoe Lake, Algonquin Park.

Artist James Edward Hervey MacDonald, co-founder of the Group of Seven, was important in Tom Thomson's life. J.E.H., as he was known, was mentor and friend. Tom and MacDonald worked together at Grip Limited and later shared meals, discussions, and painting tips in their studios in the Rosedale Valley in Toronto. J.E.H. is cited as a major influence on Tom as an artist but what is lesser known is the depth of their friendship. They helped one another in pivotal ways.

The first vignette to demonstrate their closeness concerns a cottage on Quebec Avenue in the Junction area of Toronto. No art historian has attempted to piece this tale together as sources are slight and vary significantly. Nevertheless, these meagre facts and recollections support a story

J.E.H. MacDonald, 1930, photo by M.O.Hammond, AO Digital Image I0007786.jpg.

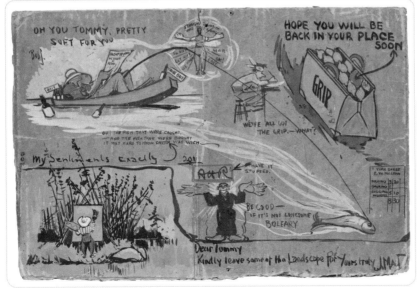

Top: *Cream of Humour,* Tom Thomson, TRL scan of image in *Tom Thomson: a Sketchbook,* Joan Murray, Art Gallery of Peel, 1996, p 30.

Bottom: *Postcard for Tom McLean,* J.E.H. MacDonald, Arts and Letters Club Archives, courtesy of Scott James, archivist.

of mutual assistance that, if accepted, illuminates the art historical narrative.

Traditional reports place Tom and J.E.H.'s first meeting at Grip Limited at the end of 1908 or the beginning of 1909, when Tom joined the firm where MacDonald was senior artist. Evidence related to the construction of the MacDonald family's first house suggests they met in 1907.

J.E.H. and his wife Joan lived in the High Park area in a rented house on Quebec Avenue[lxix] when their only child, Thoreau, was born in 1901. They left for England when Thoreau was two-years-old. In their absence, J.E.H.'s father, William Henry MacDonald, bought a plot of land in an undeveloped, wooded section of land to the north of High Park. 475 Quebec Avenue[lxx] was located in a suburban area of Toronto called the

Junction. J.E.H. and Joan loved the area, and when they returned from England, they intended to build a cottage near the wild beauties of High Park.

The MacDonald's son Thoreau retained early memories of Quebec Avenue.[lxxi] He described it as a sandy trail running through oak and red pine. There were beauteous fields of lupines, "and, among the trees, columbines, wild geraniums, anemones, hepaticas, blood root and,

Lupines J.E.H. MacDonald, 1910, PD.

under the pine shade, yellow moccasin flowers."[lxxii] Young Thoreau loved nature, like his namesake Henry David Thoreau, an author his father greatly admired.

Six-year-old Thoreau had recollections of the construction period of the new home. He noted that his father cut trees down that were in the way of the cottage's placement and that J.E.H. designed the dwelling. Sources differ about Tom Thomson's role in the design and construction. Two sources relate that J.E.H. built the cottage for Tom on MacDonald owned property—not a likely scenario.[lxxiii] The more natural conclusion is that Thomson and MacDonald worked together on the Quebec Avenue cottage intended for J.E.H. and family. In later life Thoreau remembered his father hiring a local carpenter for $500 but that hired man might well have been J.E.H.'s father. William MacDonald was a cabinet maker by trade.

Thoreau remembered too that, "While our house was building, we lived in a tent. It had a floor and was warm and I remember how the roof was weighed down by the snow." There was, no doubt, a campfire by that tent, one that allowed Tom to show off his outdoor cooking prowess. By the time the 1908 *Toronto City Directory* was printed, J.E.H. and family were listed as living in the Junction at 475 Quebec Avenue and they lived there for another two years.

Very little speculation is required to bring Tom and J.E.H. together in 1907. Legg Brothers co-worker Stuart Thompson related that Tom went sketching to the Humber River with colleagues immediately after starting work in 1905. These colleagues and their friends had been, or were, members of sketching groups such as the Toronto Art Students' League and The Mahlstick Club, organizations which had morphed into the Graphic Arts Club. All these were familiar to J.E.H.

The Graphic Arts Club went out on regular sketching trips and held "Canadian evenings" which included the robust singing of canoe songs.[lxxiv]

To contextualize the popularity of outdoor sketching in early 20th century Toronto: When J.E.H. was an apprentice at the Toronto Lithographic Co. in 1901, his boss, Joseph Thomas Rolph, sketched in a huge swath of the Greater Toronto Area. Rolph's works bore titles such as: *Scarlett's Road Near the Humber; High Park; Near Rosebank; In the Don Valley; Credit River; Yorkville Water Works; Ward's House, Toronto Island;* and *Mimico Creek.* Rolph's watercolours and oils were regularly in the Ontario Society of Artists exhibitions. J.E.H. would have been familiar with these airy outdoor scenes; he would have recognized the locations—and possibly been at them.

Top: *Lithographic Artists,* Toronto Lithographing Company Fonds, CTA, Fonds 1137, ft1137_it0014.

Lower: *Tents at High Park Sanatorium, corner of Quebec and Gothic Avenues,* TRL-SC.

Above: *Ontario Society of Artists Hanging Committee, 1927.*
Left-right: *Emanuel Hahn, Fred Haines, J.E.H. MacDonald, Dorothy Stevens, H.S. Palmer, Manley MacDonald, F.N Loverof, 1927*
Creator: J.H. Boyd Reference Code: F 1140 Item Reference Code: F 1140-7-0-2.1.

Top: *Price's Mill,*
Roxborough St. E.,
s. Side, at Price's Creek,
Rosedale, 1912,
Joseph Thomas Rolph
(1831–1916),
watercolour, TRL-SC.

Lower: J.E.H.
MacDonald. *Morning*
after Snow, High Park,
1912. Oil on canvas,
36 x 25.7 cm. Gift of
Mrs. W.D. Ross,
Toronto, 1952. © 2017
Art Gallery of Ontario.

Shortly after J.E.H. was back from England in 1907, he gravitated to Rolph's sketching areas with a special emphasis on High Park and the Humber Valley. Encouraged by his progress, J.E.H. submitted *Winter Moonlight,* and *A Hill Path—High Park* to the Ontario Society of Artists (O.S.A.) exhibition from February 22 to March 14, 1908, at the Art Gallery, 165 King Street West.

Since Tom and J.E.H. were out sketching in the same places at the same time with many of the same graphic arts colleagues, it would be odd, in fact, had they not met. Certainly by December 1907 and January 1908, as a friend, Tom would be helping J.E.H. get his family out of the snow-topped tent and into the cottage.

If one takes Tom's assistance with the Quebec Avenue cottage as fact, it goes a long way towards explaining Tom's move from Legg Brothers to Grip Limited (known variously as Grip Photoengravers, The Grip, Grip Inc., Grip Engraving Company and Grip Limited Engravers). MacDonald, as senior artist, likely helped facilitate the move for his friend. Art Director Albert Robson remembered a slicked-up Tom, in a dark blue serge suit, appearing with a portfolio and asking about an opening. "He was clean cut, almost classical in features, with a mop of black hair combed down over his right forehead. There was something intriguing about Thomson, a quiet reserve, a reticence almost approaching bashfulness. There was no bombast or assertiveness as he handed me a bundle of his work and asked if there was an opening in the art department."[lxxv] By January 1909, Tom was definitely working at Grip Limited.

Brown Betty Tea Room, photo in "Brown Betty's *Eighteenth Birthday*", *The Globe*, Toronto, February 26, 1926, TRL, Newspaper Room.

During the next five years, the friends grew closer, sharing more than a meal or two in Toronto. Their discussions centered not just on what Canadian art should look like, but also, on the difficulties of making a living as a professional artist. They probably met at the Brown Betty Tea Room on King Street East, the locale favoured by the men of the Arts and Letters Club. J.E.H. had taken an interest in the Club when it opened in 1908, and by 1911 he was a member and had a successful exhibition there. The Brown Betty[lxxvi] featured a diversified menu, boasted the best chicken in town and smoking was permitted, a good thing as Tom was rarely without pipes and Hudson Bay tobacco.

A second vignette further shows the bond between Tom and J.E.H. In 1912, MacDonald left Grip Limited to make it on his own as a professional artist. He bought a house in Thornhill. J.E.H. discovered immediately that he had to take commissions to keep the new roof over his family's heads. In 1913 he took on a contract for the Toronto General Hospital Board. He was to design and illustrate a leather-bound album to be presented to the Lieutenant Governor, Sir John Morison Gibson, for the official opening of the hospital in June 1913. J.E.H. was also to produce a pamphlet showing the hospital's new operating rooms and equipment. The project was massive and had a short deadline. MacDonald called on Stanley Kemp, a former Grip Limited co-worker, to help.

Desperation set in just before the printer's deadline. J.E.H. needed extra hands to get the job done. J.E.H. called Tom who dropped everything and rushed to Thornhill via the radial railroad. Kemp described the scene: "I can still see MacDonald and me standing as reception committee, watching the last radial car come down the hill and then up the hill and then blessed relief, Tommy Thomson getting off as promised. Three pairs of hands being pumped like pump handles."[lxxvii]

MacDonald's son Thoreau, then 12-years-old, peeked at the men as they worked all that night. He knew that Tom had had great adventures in the north the past summer.

> *"I hung around hoping to hear something about the North, but can only recollect Tom smiling and working quietly."*

The trio met the deadline. Tom gave Stanley Kemp, the *Marsh, Lake Scugog*, 1911, as a gift in the fall of 1913. Just as Tom had most likely helped MacDonald speed up the completion of the Quebec Avenue cottage, he stepped in six years later when his friend needed him for the Toronto General Hospital contract. J.E.H. had returned the favour when he introduced

Tom to Dr. James MacCallum who in 1913 guaranteed Tom's expenses for a year so that Tom could further develop his artistic talents.

Early in 1914, both Tom and MacDonald moved into The Studio Building where they had even more time together. When J.E.H. commuted from Thornhill to Studio Six, young Thoreau MacDonald liked to go along. Tom was very fond of children. He'd had three younger siblings while growing up, two nephews in Seattle and he visited his Harkness and Gilchrist nephews and nieces when they lived in the Owen Sound area. Additionally, Thoreau MacDonald was Tom's kind of lad: quiet, well read, interested in graphic design, philosophical and passionate about nature. Thoreau's 1912 journal[lxxviii] demonstrates his observational skills of everything from snails and snakes to birds.

Toronto General Hospital (opened 1913), College St., s. Side, between Elizabeth St. & University Avenue, TRL Baldwin Collection.

Diet Kitchen, illustration in Private Patients' Building / Toronto General Hospital, an unpaginated booklet printed by Grip Limited, Toronto for W.G. Macfarlane Ltd. ca. 1913, Toronto General.

Hospital fonds, Board of Trustees records, Special Events and Ceremonies, TG 1.6.12, University Health Network Archives, Toronto.

Tom Thomson, J.E.H. and Stanley Kemp worked on these drawings for the TGH.

An Operating Room, illustration in Private Patients' Building / Toronto General Hospital, an unpaginated booklet printed by Grip Limited, Toronto for W.G. Macfarlane Ltd. ca. 1913, Toronto.

General Hospital fonds, Board of Trustees records, Special Events and Ceremonies, TG 1.6.12, University Health Network Archives, Toronto.

Toronto General Hospital

Single Room with Bath, illustration in Private Patients' Building / Toronto General Hospital, an unpaginated booklet printed by Grip Limited, Toronto for W.G. Macfarlane Ltd. ca. 1913, Toronto.

General Hospital fonds, Board of Trustees records, Special Events and Ceremonies, TG 1.6.12, University Health Network Archives, Toronto.

Three Room Suite, illustration in Private Patients' Building / Toronto General Hospital, an unpaginated booklet printed by Grip Limited, Toronto for W.G. Macfarlane Ltd. ca. 1913, Toronto.

General Hospital fonds, Board of Trustees records, Special Events and Ceremonies, TG 1.6.12, University Health Network Archives, Toronto.

the trio met the deadline

"Too much Mulligan".

A.L. 1915

Left: *Arthur Lismer "Too Much Mulligan", 1915*
graphite on wove paper, 19.7 x 25.4 cm.
Gift of the artist, Montreal, before 1946
National Gallery of Canada, Ottawa Photo.

Right: *Arthur Lismer Shack at No. 25 Severn Street, Toronto, 1915*
graphite on wove paper, 25.3 x 19.5 cm.
Gift of the artist, Montreal, before 1946
National Gallery of Canada, Ottawa Photo.

Drawings by Arthur Lismer

When Tom moved into The Shack, Thoreau did too— on his visits. Thoreau watched Tom paint and carve axe handles, and of course, cook.

"Seeing my interest in the axe handles he very characteristically gave me a couple and I have one of them still."

Thoreau MacDonald, Appendix to Ottelyn Addison's *Tom Thomson the Algonquin Years,* p 85

A Dutch oven habitually simmered mulligan stew— Tom's Shack staple. A 1915 drawing by Arthur Lismer shows Tom slumped in a chair from

Too Much Mulligan.

"Brown Betty's Eighteenth Birthday", *The Globe,* Toronto, February 26, 1926.

"Tom Thomson's iron range, from memory", Thoreau MacDonald illustration in article by Paul Duval, from *Telegram* column "Accent on Art", September 1, 1962.

Thoreau recalled the iron range Tom had for cooking, the flourish with which he threw a handful of tea into the pot, "and mashed the potatoes with an empty bottle, adding what looked like half a pound of butter." Tom also had a stock of his homemade preserves which he told Thoreau he couldn't leave as they'd freeze if the fire went out. Thoreau said, "He had canned these from berries brought down from the North."

A portrait Tom painted of Thoreau, subsequently titled "Day Dreaming", shows the special relationship between them. The lanky 13-year-old lies in a farm field looking at Tom. There is curiosity and trust in his gaze.

When Tom died, he left approximately 300 works in The Shack. Sixteen-year-old Thoreau helped J.E.H. classify and stamp the works. They sorted them onto tall shelves under headings such as snow, sunsets and the seasons. It was a labour of love.

Cottage on Quebec Avenue, one of the few bungalows on the street.

65

The Food Connection

—posited on co-building the Quebec Avenue cottage

In the winter of 1907 as Tom and J.E.H. worked on the Quebec Avenue cottage, a campfire for heat, tea and flapjacks, was kept going. Tom was known for his masterful pancakes. He also might have brought his own strawberry preserves and homemade maple syrup to slather on them—treats for young Thoreau.

Placing Tom and J.E.H. inside the Brown Betty Tea Rooms is speculative, yet plausible. Three sisters, who were nurses, opened the tearooms in February 1908. The next month, a group of men met above the restaurant to discuss founding the Arts and Letters Club. For two years after its founding, the Arts and Letters Club brought its meals upstairs directly from the tea rooms below them. When the Brown Betty moved one door east on King Street in 1910, Augustus Bridle plotted to put a hole in the wall to construct a dumb waiter. The landlord caught on and gave the group the boot.

The Brown Betty's spacious new setting and cozy decor made it an easier go-to place than the finer McConkey's Restaurant Tom visited with his sister Minnie. It's easy to imagine Tom and J.E.H. in the Men's Luncheon Room of Brown Betty's eating the chicken special—quite a step up from Tom's boring boarding house meals.

In terms of Tom's cooking, Thoreau MacDonald mentioned mulligan stew. I went off in search for its history. The term mulligan first appeared at the turn of the 19th century, usually to describe a brew concocted in a heavy iron pot with items found, begged, scavenged or stolen. Mulligans were identified as Irish, community, beef or hobo stews. American hobos made community stews in which the meat was anything from squirrel, opossum and chicken to beef and lamb— even occasionally fish. The starch came from potatoes or stale bread and the vegetables were anything available, usually root vegetables. Hobo seasoning tended to be just salt and pepper, but in Tom's Shack, anything that was dried, or that he'd brought back from his father's kitchen garden was added for flavour.

Tom had lots of friends in The Studio Building to supply mulligan ingredients: John Beatty, Studio Four; Curtis Williamson, Studio Five; Arthur Heming, Studio Three; J.E.H. MacDonald, Studio Six; Lawren Harris, Studio Two; and Franklin Carmichael with him in Studio One. With all those pals to throw something into the pot, no wonder there was often "too much mulligan"!

The unattributed recipe below is less collaborative than the concoctions of The Shack.

Mulligan Stew

½ cup each of diced onions, carrots, celery and turnip;

4 potatoes quartered;

Add to ⅛ lb. salt pork,

2 pounds venison, lamb or beef cut in small pieces and cooked 1 hour in 1 pint of water

1 teaspoon salt and ¼ tsp. Pepper

Cook all together for one hour

Dumplings to taste may be added last 12 minutes.

Turning my inquisitive mind to Tom's preserves, I found an easy jam recipe that would work well on the trail. Tom wouldn't have weighed the berries as in the jam recipe in *Toronto (Queen City of Canada) Cookbook.* He'd have found another way to ensure equal quantities. He'd also have swapped his Dutch kettle and a bottle for mashing. (Thoreau described Tom mashing potatoes with a bottle.) At Quebec Avenue or on the trail, the jam might well have gone with flapjacks or oatmeal.

Raspberry and Blackberry Jam

"Pick over berries and weigh them. Mash a few in the bottom of a preserving kettle with a wooden potato masher and so continue until the fruit is all used. Heat slowly to boiling point and add gradually their weight of heated sugar. Cook slowly 45 minutes, then put in stone jars or tumblers."

Belles of Leith, back row second from left, Minnie Thomson and fourth from left, Louisa Thomson. GRM, WIF63-2-002.

Belles of Leith

CHAPTER SEVEN

Fine and Farm Dining, Minnie Thomson Henry

Minnie and Tom Thomson were literally in diapers together. She was born in 1875 and he in 1877. They spent almost 20 years together as their youth on the farm in Leith was attenuated by the terms of their grandfather Tam Thomson's will. The Thomson brothers and sisters in their turns decamped at 21-years-of-age with their inheritance—the young men to study and work and the young women usually to marry. Minnie, one of the 'Belles of Leith' was still single at 28-years-of-age.

Minnie put aside her inheritance as a dowry in 1896. Then in 1904, the bright-eyed 28-year-old "Miss" spent a part of this dowry to enrol in the Demill Ladies' College in the Yates Street area of St. Catharines. Minnie headed off to study, "Classics, Modern Languages, Natural Sciences, Elocution and Voice Culture, Commercial Forms, Music, Art, Ornamental Work and Physical Training." The Demill College in St. Catharines included these courses in its three year programs.

Minnie wrote Blodwen Davies February 2, 1931, "After Tom returned from Seattle, I saw less of him than other members of the family who were at home, as I was away a good deal. At the time of his return I was in St. Catherines [sic] and missed his visit." He was at work at his $11 [soon to be $15] a week position at Legg Brothers in Toronto.

Minnie and Tom planned a fall weekend visit. Minnie wrote in the same letter to Davies, "… he took a weekend to come across on the boat from Toronto, to see me, and we had a most satisfying visit together. That was in the fall of 1905."

William Cruikshank, *Sand Wagon*, 1895 oil on canvas, 91.6 x 132.4 cm Royal Canadian Academy of Arts diploma work, deposited by the artist, Toronto, 1895 National Gallery of Canada, Ottawa Photo.

[1] Tom Thomson (1877–1917) *Farmer Leading Two Horses* around 1907 oil on canvas 28.5 x 38.5 cm. From the Estate of Thomas James Gibson Henry [nephew of Tom Thomson], on perpetual loan to the Tom Thomson Art Gallery, Owen Sound, from the Ontario Heritage Trust, an agency of the Government of Ontario.

[1] *Tom Thomson was obviously experimenting with a popular theme when he painted his team of horses.*

Top Left: *Tom Thomson Lock, Welland (?) Canal,* c. *1905* graphite on wove paper, 20.9 x 12.5 cm Gift of Leanora D. McCarney, Hull, Quebec, 1990 National Gallery of Canada, Ottawa Photo.

Top Right: *Steamer "Lakeside" Leaving Port Dalhousie,* postcard, PD.

STEAMER "LAKESIDE" LEAVING PORT DALHOUSIE, ONT.

1708

Lower Right: *Tom Thomson Hotel (?) on a Hill,* c. 1905 graphite on wove paper, 12.5 x 20.9 cm Gift of Leanora D. McCarney, Hull, Quebec, 1990 National Gallery of Canada, Ottawa Photo.

Lower Left: *Welland Ship Canal – Old Welland Canal and Ridley College, St. Catharines,* Francis J. Petrie Collection D420318, Niagara Falls Public Library.

Harvest Scene John William Beatty PD.

Tom would have boarded the Lake Ontario, wooden-propeller steamship, *Lakeside* to get to St. Catharines. For two decades this popular ship made daily, round trips between Toronto and Port Dalhousie. Captain N. J. Wigle delivered up to 300 passengers to the electric-powered rail cars that transported them to St. Catharines and Niagara Falls. Two sketches in Tom's leather-bound sketch book may now be identified. *Lock, Welland (?) Canal, 1905* in the National Gallery of Canada is lock number one of the Welland Canal and *Hotel (?) on a Hill* is a view of Ridley College from the river.

The image of Tom Thomson hanging over the railing of a Lake Ontario steamer, his face into the wind, seems to be one for the imagination. Yet, based on family recollection it's a likely image. Louisa wrote Miss Davies on March 11, 1931, "As far back as I can remember Tom was fond of drawing and so often his pictures were of a sailing vessel with sails set to the breeze …." Louisa goes on to describe a sail boat race during a stiff breeze on the bay at Leith. Tom and David Ross raced Joe Coture's two-masted fishing boat and won. Tom would have enjoyed his Lake Ontario ship travel.

Tom Thomson *St. Thomas Church, St. Catharines*, c. 1905 graphite on wove paper, 20.9 x 12.5 cm Gift of Leanora D. McCarney, Hull, Quebec, 1990 National Gallery of Canada, Ottawa Photo.

On the fall 1905 weekend excursion to St. Catharines, Tom accompanied Minnie to church—first to worship and then to sketch. Minnie related, "While he was there he and I attended St. Thomas Church, and next morning he made a rough sketch of it." Minnie praised his pencil drawing before he headed back to catch the *Lakeside* to Toronto. She wrote, "On Christmas of 1906 he gave me a large water color sketch of this church, I have it still, and it is one of the most admired and prized of all my pictures." – and no wonder! It was a memento of their special time together.

Life headed down new paths for Minnie and Tom shortly thereafter. Tom learned about evening courses at the Central Toronto School of Art and Design. It seemed most of his sketching pals took courses with William Cruikshank and thus, Tom worked in time for lessons with the senior artist. The legendary teacher of painting from plaster casts complimented Tom's oil painting of a man leading two horses. Tom told his sisters that Cruikshank had looked at the work and said, "Well, you'd better keep on. His teacher's [William Cruikshank] comment was his first real encouragement: "Did you paint this? Well, you'd better keep on."[1]

It was a heady moment that set Tom to thinking seriously about his art. It was one thing to be good with lettering, decorative design and the Ben Day Shading[lxxix] machine, another to create fine art.

[1] *Ottelyn Addison, Tom Thomson: The Algonquin Years,* p 4 caption.

Minnie had a new path to consider as well. On a trip home in 1906, her sister Louisa indicated she would marry neighbour James Henry in February of 1907 and that his brother William was interested in her. Minnie still had the third year of Demill courses to complete but the thought of heading west with her sister was tempting. Tom knew the Henry men from growing up with them in Leith but he'd also spent time with them during his years in Seattle. Minnie had the opportunity to discuss the marriage proposal and the prospects with Tom on a visit to Toronto. He had invited her.

Happy with developments in his Toronto life, Tom encouraged Minnie to stop by after she'd finished Demill that year. He took her to work at Legg Brothers and introduced her to each of the four members of the design team, explaining each person's individual functions.

Then he escorted his favourite sister for a special lunch at McConkey's Restaurant.

The Palm Garden at McConkey's Restaurant, King Street West, 1899,
photo from Marilyn M. Litvak,
Edward James Lennox: Builder of Toronto, p 64. Source TRL.

Henry Family Album, photos TFC:

Top Left: Gibson, Minnie and Louisa.

Top Right: Louisa and Minnie in Washington.

Lower Right: Louisa, Gibson's wife, Minnie and Gibson Henry.

Henry Family Album

Although there were several manifestations of Mc-Conkey eating establishments from the 1840s to the 1940s, Minnie specifically said in her letter to Davies, "He knew the most delightful tea rooms, and one day he took me to McKonkey's [sic]. I had not been there before, and remarked on what a delightful place it was, how cool and restful, and on the beautiful service and delicious food." The McConkey's Minnie described was likely the restaurant on King Street. Its elegant dining room was the first Toronto location lit by electricity. The spark that started in 1889, when one electrode jumped to another, had not fizzled out. People still longed for the finery of McConkey's. According to Minnie, Tom admired the atmosphere and the fine people. He'd said,

> *"I would eat here always, but one can't on $15 a week."*

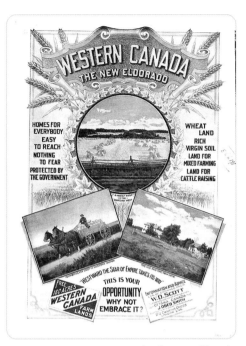

Western Canada, the new Eldorado, LAC, C-085854 and Free Homes for the Millions, LAC, C-095320.

When Minnie arrived home to Owen Sound that July of 1907, she'd made up her mind to marry William Henry. There were many possibilities for free or inexpensive farmland in the west. There was even a book published in 1907 titled *The Last Best West: Canada in the Twentieth Century (Western Canada) vast Agricultural Resources, homes for millions.*[lxxx] The west beckoned.

The members of the quartet of potential husbands and wives were then over 30-years-of-age. The sisters had the cash to grubstake and the skills to homestead, whereas William and James were experienced farmers. In 1907, the brothers were helping their widowed mother, Janet Gibson Henry, who still had several of her 12 children at home at the farm in Leith. It was time for Minnie, Louisa, William and James to seize destiny.

Bird's Eye View of Pense, Sask. Postcard PCO11322, Prairie Postcards Collection, Peel Library, University of Alberta.

William Henry, photo, Ancestry.ca.

Minnie and William married December 27, 1907 and, to be sure, Tom danced with his favourite sister on her wedding day. To Minnie's surprise, for a gift, Tom gave her the oil painting of the man leading the horses. Minnie was delighted, as she knew how important that painting had been to Tom's sense of his developing skill as an artist.

Early in 1908, as Tom worked on the construction of J.E.H.'s cottage on Quebec Avenue, Minnie, Louisa, James and William headed west to farm in Pense, Saskatchewan, and then later in 1912, on neighbouring farms in Guernsey. Tom's nephew Thomas Gibson Henry[lxxxi] was born to Minnie and William in December 1912 when Minnie was 37-years-old.

Tom had had the opportunity to see his brothers-in-law William and James Henry in the months before the birth of this baby. When William's and James' mother, Janet, died in Guernsey on September 21, 1912, they accompanied her body back to the Leith Cemetery to be laid beside their father. The Henry brothers met up with Tom and William Smithson Broadhead in Owen Sound. Tom and work pal Broadhead were recently back from a two month adventure in the wild Mississagi region. The pair talked excitedly about fishing, foraging, paddling, rain and painting. Tom told his brothers-in-law of friendly encounters with big black bears and large timber wolves.

Minnie saw her brother Fraser when he visited them out west in October of 1915. She saw Tom in November 1915, when the two sisters visited Owen Sound with toddler Gibson Henry in tow. Minnie noticed Tom was much more serious, "engrossed in his art."

She never saw her favourite brother again.

Henry family on the porch in Saskatchewan, photo. From left: Louisa, James, unidentified lady, Gibson, Minnie and William Henry. TFC.

In 1922, the two Henry families moved to Aberdeen, Saskatchewan, where they were part of the congregation of the United Church. In 1927, the ladies of the church assembled a cook book for fund raising purposes. Minnie and Louisa contributed seven recipes. Although the recipes were recorded a decade after Tom's death, they provide insight into the baking and cooking Tom would have learned in the Thomson household in Leith. It's the best chance, you'll ever have, to cook food that Tom Thomson likely ate while growing up.

The Food Connection

The 1927 recipes Minnie and Louisa contributed to their church's fundraiser show basics of pioneer cooking. Minnie's beefsteak pie was sure to be a Tom Thomson staple, perhaps even made with black squirrels.

Reliable Recipes: compiled by Mrs. J. Wilkinson, Mrs. M. Staples, Mrs. W. Wilkinson, Mrs. J. MacLennan, Talent Money for Ladies' Aid 1927 of United Church, Aberdeen, Saskatchewan, Pastor, Rev. H.A. Macmanus in *Aberdeen 1907–1981,* Aberdeen, Aberdeen Historical Society 1982, pp 293–306 (originally 52 pages) These recipes are presented as they appeared, without corrections.

Parker House Rolls,
Mrs. J. G. (Louisa) Henry p 294

"Soak 1 yeast cake in a little warm water till soft, take 3 cups warm milk, $\frac{2}{3}$ cups sugar, or more if desired, scant $\frac{1}{2}$ cup butter, 1 teaspoon salt; put in yeast and mix together, knead in enough warm flour to make a rather soft dough that will not stick to the hands, knead well and cover closely; let rise till morning, then work down three times, each time let dough double its bulk; cut in any desired shape, dip in melted butter, put cream and sugar on top. Put 1 inch apart in pans and let rise till very light. Bake 25 minutes in bread oven."

Caramel Pie,
Mrs. Wm. (Minnie) Henry p 297

"Burn 2 tablespoons sugar on pan till dark brown, then pour on $\frac{3}{4}$ cup water and let boil off. Scald 2 cups milk, add 3 rounded tablespoons corn starch, cook thoroughly, 1 heaping cup brown sugar, burn sugar syrup, yolks of 3 eggs well beaten, a piece of butter and vanilla. Beat whites for top or use whipped cream."

Dried Beef,
Mrs. Wm. (Minnie) Henry p 301

"Take the ham of a young beef preferably, and for every 20 lbs. Use 1 pt. Salt, $\frac{1}{4}$ teaspoons saltpetre, 1 lb. Brown sugar, 1 teaspoon ground cloves, 1 teaspoon allspice. Trim the piece of beef neatly, after the spices have been rubbed well together, divide into 3 equal parts and rub well into the beef for 3 consecutive days. Push in and rub an extra handful of salt into the hole for string and around the bone. Keep in a vessel or large platter and turn the meat every day in the liquor it will make. In 4 or 5 days hang in a cool, dry place, where it will only drip for a few hours. Very delicious fried in plenty of butter."

Beefsteak Pie,
Mrs. Wm. (Minnie) Henry p 302

"Put a layer of fried steak in a deep dish, cover with slightly thickened gravy, seasoned; add a layer of sliced onions and fill dish with finely sliced onions. Season all with salt and pepper, and dot with butter. Cover and bake like escalloped potatoes."

Beefsteak,
Mrs. J. G. (Louisa) Henry p 302

"Take a quantity of beefsteak cut rather thick, pound into it all the flour it will take, fry quickly in butter or beef fat, then cover with boiling water. Cover closely and simmer on back of range from 1 to 1½ hours. 15 minutes before lifting, thicken gravy and season well with salt and pepper."

Sweet Tomato Pickle,
Mrs. J. G. (Louisa) Henry p 303

"1 peck green tomatoes, 6 large onions sliced. Sprinkle with salt overnight, drain and add 2 qts. Vinegar, 1 qt. Water, boil 15 minutes; add 2 lbs. sugar, 2 tablespoons cloves, allspice, ginger, ground mustard, cinnamon mixed. 1 teaspoon red pepper. Boil 15 minutes and seal hot."

French Salad,
Mrs. W. (Minnie) Henry p 304

"To 1 pt. canned peas add 1 pt. chopped celery, 1 cup chopped walnuts, ½ cups chopped orange. Serve with mayonnaise dressing on shredded lettuce; garnish with olives or pimentos."

Now's your chance! Cook and eat like Tom Thomson.

1921 Armstrong Kitchen, antiquehomestyle.com PD.

Prairie Kitchen, PD.

Left: Tom Thomson (1877–1917) *Fairy Lake 1912,* oil on paperboard, 17.7 x 22.7 cm. Gift of the Founders, Robert and Signe McMichael, through the good offices of Mrs. Edgar Burke, Swift Current, Saskatchewan. McMichael Canadian Art Collection. 1966.16.63.

Right: *Fairy Lake,* pencil, 1875, George Harlow White, TRL-SC, JRR 3026.

{excerpt from the *Huntsville Forester*, Thursday, July 26, 1906}

GRAND TRUNK RY.

G. T. R. STATION STAFF.

Back row, from left to right—C. P. Hines, Day Assistant; E. Burke, Baggageman; J. E. Thompson, Night Assistant. Front row, from left to right—W. S. Jones, Day Operator; Philip Meyer, Agent; J. G. Oliver, Night Operator.

Above: *Gerrard Street, north east side, 1912,* TRL, TEC 503B. It would have looked like this when Tom lived at 99 Gerrard Street.

Right: *Excerpt. Huntsville Forester,* Thursday July 26, 1906. Edgar Burke is middle back.

CHAPTER EIGHT

Picnic at Fairy Lake, Edgar Burke and Family

Handsome Edgar Francis Burke was a 20-year-old Grand Trunk baggage man in 1906 when he posed for a photo with his fellow railroad employees in Huntsville,[lxxxii] Edgar's father was John Thomas Burke, captain of the 52 metre long schooner, the *Myron Butman*.[lxxxiii] The American schooner had a wooden hull and three masts, as well as mechanical power, to ply the waters of the Great Lakes in the lumber trade. The captain's family lived in a gracious home[lxxxiv] at One Lansdowne Street West in Huntsville, on the hill behind the Dominion Hotel.

Captain Burke had retired from his career on lake ships by 1908; he ran a grocery store east of the bridge in Huntsville. Edgar's older brother Anson advertised himself in the Huntsville *Forester* as "Anson G. Burke, Druggist and Optical". With his father and brother settled in livelihoods, Edgar let ambition take him to Toronto.

He was going to be more than a railroad baggage man. The January 16, 1908, edition of the Huntsville *Forester* reported, "Edgar Burke went to Toronto on Thursday last to take a Business College Course."

In Toronto, Edgar lodged at 99 Gerrard Street at the north-eastern edge of the impoverished "Ward" district that teemed with new immigrants. Esther Varty Plewes was doyenne of the large and busy boarding establishment at that location. The widow Plewes[1] was nearly 61-years-old in 1908, and had adult children, their spouses and a spate of grandchildren living with her. To maximize income from boarders, Esther housed up to 15 of them at the same time. The *1911 Census of Canada* recorded 26 men and women living at that address during the course of that year—now that's a full house! The list of the boarders' occupations is a snapshot of working life in urban

---

[1] Tom gifted *Summer Landscape, 1911* to Mrs. Plewes.

Top Left: *Winnie Trainor and class at St. Joseph Academy 1903,* MHPC, Huntsville, Ontario 1970.610 Winnie is in last row, second from left.

Centre Right: "Landsdowne Street Home of Captain Burke", photo. *Pictures from the Past, Huntsville,* Research Committee of Muskoka Pioneer Village, p 115. Thanks to Muskoka Room of Huntsville Public Library.

Lower Right: *Lansdowne Home of the Burke Family,* current photo, Angie Littlefield.

Canada 30 years after Confederation: brass engraver, glass worker, fur finisher, ticket seller, milliner (there were three), stenographer, cook, druggist, foreman, manager and of course our Thomas Thomson, listed as a designer.[lxxxv]

Edgar Burke, the sociable young man from Huntsville, fit well into this crowded milieu. He noted the comings and goings in the busy household. In 1909, when 32-year-old Tom Thomson arrived, Edgar scouted out the tall, quiet man.

Thomson worked at a company called Grip Limited, went on sketching excursions with interesting friends, painted in his room and seemed happy to have flown a nest of loud evangelists at previous lodgings.

Whenever Edgar wandered into the clouds of pipe smoke to look at Tom paint or draw, he admired works he saw lying around. Invariably, Tom would give the chatty young man what he admired and Edgar would leave with his spoils. In that way Edgar acquired a 1903 watercolour of a lady drawing a bow, a sketch of a proposed design for a stained glass window, and an oil painting of a sailboat.[lxxxvi] Tom parted easily with the works, wondering why young Edgar wanted them.

Edgar also received a pen-and-ink sketch of a fisherman, for which he later claimed he'd posed one rainy Sunday afternoon in Huntsville. The story of Edgar posing for that sketch is likely, as Tom went to Huntsville for fishing, hunting and for visits with his friends John and Edythe McRuer. There's even the remote possibility that Tom knew Edgar from Huntsville. Tom had been there many times and may have met Edgar the Grand Trunk baggage man; he may have shopped in Captain Burke's store or made purchases at Anson Burke's Pharmacy.

Background image, Muskoka River.

85

Far Left: *Tom Thomson, (Canadian, 1877–1917), Old Lake Captain,* 1908, 60.96x 35.56 cm, oil on canvas; masonite, Gift of Colonel Eric Phillips, The Beaverbrook Art Gallery, Fredericton, NB, Canada.

Centre: *Captain Raoul Lalonde standing beside the wheelhouse of the Montreal & Cornwall Navigation Company steamboat BRITANNIC.* www.MaritimeHistoryOfTheGreatLakes.ca.

Lower Right: *Myron Butman, 1885, photo, C. Patrick Labadie Collection / Thunder Bay National Marine Sanctuary, Alpena, Michigan. John Thomas Burke was captain of the wooden hulled lumber schooner Samuel J. Tilden 1899–1900 and then took the helm of the Myron Butman 1905–1908.*

Tom Thomson (bow), Margaret McRuer, Edyth McRuer's sister, Bertie Chambers, Dr. John McRuer and wife Edyth (stern). Gift of Katherine McIntyre, McMichael Canadian Art Collection Archives. The working theory of this chapter is that the photo shows Tom Thomson at front with the child, Anson Burke partially obscured by his wife Opel, Matilda Burke in the middle; at the rear Edgar and Frances Floss (later Burke).

The early Thomson work titled *Portrait of an Old Lake Captain,* may indeed portray Edgar's father. Captain Burke had recently retired from a career on the Great Lakes and kept connected to his maritime life as a supplier of ship's provisions.[lxxxvii] The captain's wistful view from the dock may be interpreted as the portrayal of a man searching for former glories. Since Tom tended to portray landscapes, not persons, when he did take on a portrait, the person was frequently linked to his life. It seems reasonable that the old Lake Captain might indeed be John Thomas Burke.

In 1910 when Edgar was done with his courses in Toronto, he was offered a job as a residential engineer with the Canadian National Railway. Edgar left to live part time with an uncle in Calgary while the CNR built its way towards that city.[lxxxviii] When Edgar visited the town of Swift Current,[1] Saskatchewan, a town of 600 residents, he met the beautiful Frances A. Floss and fell in love. In 1912, with Edgar's employee rail privileges, the couple visited Huntsville at the same time Tom Thomson visited.

Nearly the whole Burke family turned out for an excursion to Fairy Lake with Tom Thomson. A photo of the outing said to show the McRuers, probably shows Tom in a boat with Edgar and Frances, Edgar's brother Anson and his wife Opel, and an older woman, Edgar's mother, Matilda Burke, the well-loved humanitarian of Huntsville.[lxxxix] Matilda lived to be 101-years-old but was just entering her fifth decade at that point. After a great time fishing and picnicking, Tom decided on a gift for the Burkes. He arrived at the Lansdowne Street house to present Edgar with a freshly painted oil of Fairy Lake—one he'd painted from a sketch at his lodgings in the Dominion Hotel.

[1] *The Huntsville lawyer, Samuel Albert Hutcheson also settled in Swift Current and Anson and Opel moved there as well.*

In a September 8, 1963, article in the Swift Current newspaper, *The Sun,* Frances Burke recalled a story about the painting*:*

"You didn't sign it," Mr. Burke said to Thomson, and the artist, eager to please his friend, scratched the now-familiar 'Tom Thomson' into the fresh oil with the point of a hastily found pin."

Frances Burke also recalled that Tom wrote them in 1916 to apologize he'd not been able to afford a wedding present. He offered instead to paint their Swift Current home at 270, 5th Avenue when he made it there on a trip he was planning to the west. In 1917, Edgar and Frances Burke were very sorry to hear that he'd never make it.[xc]

Tom and Edgar Burke's friendship was not a long one. They shared meals together at Esther Plewes' crowded boarding house and possibly in restaurants nearby such as Jack and Jill's Café or the Chinese restaurant at Pembroke and Queen Streets that Tom and Elizabeth McCarnen had frequented. Edgar and Tom also had time together in Huntsville. Tom was close enough to Edgar to be invited to his wedding.

Tom may also have kept up the friendship with Edgar's parents, Captain and Mrs. Burke, when Edgar went west. The elder Burkes were popular and very hospitable. Tom had lots of reasons to visit Huntsville—the McRuers and the Burkes, fishing and hunting parties, great sites for painting and starting in 1913, another tantalizing reason: Winnifred Trainor. Winnifred grew up near the Burkes and her family had a cabin on Canoe Lake. Huntsville was indeed a very attractive place!

The Food Connection

Tom's probable trip with the Burkes to Fairy Lake in 1912 provided the perfect opportunity to look into the food conventions of picnics in the 1900s. Fairy Lake was a resort adjoining Huntsville; it had boat rental places with food concessions where the group could have stocked up. I considered what the group might have purchased at these concessions (Hot dogs? Ice cream? Sandwiches?) Then I decided it was more fun to guess what Frances, Opel and Matilda Burke brought along for the picnic at Fairy Lake.

Fairy Lake, photo Angie Littlefield.

A period cook book, *The Economy Administration Cook Book*, edited by Susie Root Rhodes and Grace Porter Hopkins (Hammond IN, W.B. Conkey Co., 1913) suggests six different picnic menus:

"The Box Lunch:

No. 1: Two Roast Beef Sandwiches, One Tomato Sandwich, Two Stalks of Celery (heart), Six or eight Dates stuffed with Nuts and Ginger.

No. 2: Chopped Egg Sandwiches (two), One Lettuce Sandwich, Four Raisin Cookies.

No. 3: Two Cream Cheese and Red Pepper Sandwiches (made of brown bread), One cup Fruit Gelatin, Two Sponge Cakes.

No. 4: Four slices of plain Bread and Butter, One small jar of Meat Salad, Two Fruit Turnovers.

No. 5: Two slices Graham Bread and Lemon Butter, Two slices of crisp Bacon, One minced Ham Sandwich, Two slices of Raisin Loaf, One Apple.

No. 6: Two Chicken Sandwiches, One Currant Jelly Sandwich, Two Stalks Celery (heart), Raisins and Nuts." (p. 229)

NOTE: The box or wrapped lunch should be most carefully planned and prepared. Provision should be made, if possible, to reheat some dish or to purchase a hot one to supplement that which is carried. Have ready *paraffine* paper for wrapping, a folding box, a screw top bottle for milk, cocoa or soup, a covered cup or jar for soft materials, such as custards, salads or jellies."

There was lots of variety for menu planning in the Rhodes and Hopkins book. The quantities would have had to be larger for a boatload of adults. I wondered too if the French–Canadian influence of Matilda Burke (born Matilda Clouthier in Quebec) made its way into the picnic hamper? *Soupe aux pois*? *Tourtière*? *Tarte au sucre*?

What was on the menu for Tom Thomson's déjeuner sur l'herbe at Fairy Lake?

MISS WINNIE TRAINOR
HUNTSVILLE ONT.

PICTURE TAKEN IN THE EARLY 1900

Left: *Winnifred Trainor, known as Winnie, 1900*, MHPC, Huntsville, Ontario 1962.17.1.

Top Right: *"Group Conversing, 1911" The Star*, May 20, 1912 p. 8 . CTA, Fonds 1244, Item 560. Millinery was a definite 'thing' in the early 1900s.

Lower Right: *Shore leave at Imbros.* Three midshipmen set off for an afternoon's picnic, carrying a basket and a kettle. Image from Australian War Memorial on lemnosgallipolicc.blogspot.ca. Always time for a picnic, even during the Battle of Gallipoli!

Hats and Picnics

Canoe Lake photo Angie Littlefield

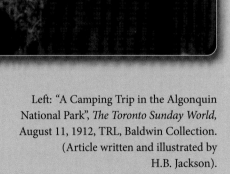

Left: "A Camping Trip in the Algonquin National Park", *The Toronto Sunday World*, August 11, 1912, TRL, Baldwin Collection. (Article written and illustrated by H.B. Jackson).

Right: *Harry Jackson*, Tom Thomson, photo. Compare photo to image of pipe-smoking Harry at left in the newspaper article.

CHAPTER NINE

Call Me Harry, Henry Benson Jackson

" ▪ ▪ ▪ there's no more pleasant time than when the cookee lifts the boiling, good-smelling kettles off the wangan over the fire, and you sit down to eat and eat." H.B. Jackson *Toronto Sunday World*, August 11, 1912.

When Tom Thomson fell in love with Algonquin Park in 1912, he was with Harry Jackson.[xci] Both paddled over Canoe Lake, threw out their fishing lines at Tea Lake Dam and looked up at stormy spring skies over Smoke Lake for the first time that May. Very little is known about the man who shared these pivotal first moments with Canada's most prominent painter.

Harry's letters to Thomson biographer Blodwen Davies, the article he wrote and illustrated for *The Toronto Sunday World* in 1912, and his obituary in the *Monroe Evening News* in 1953, form a better picture of the mysterious Harry and of this important first visit that changed the direction of Tom Thomson's life.

Harry Jackson was born in Waltham, Massachusetts, in 1871. Before he arrived at the Grip Limited in 1910, the 39-year-old had studied and worked in Boston, New York, and Chicago. Art Director Albert Robson hired the bespectacled Harry as an experienced tourism publicity specialist. Harry was a senior man in the Grip Limited workroom.

Once Harry settled into a boarding house towards the south of tree-lined Jarvis Street,[xcii] he began looking for friends. A few sketching trips later, he'd decided on Tom Thomson, the man who was contemplative one moment, and in the next, sprang to the centre of the party playing his mandolin. Harry told Blodwen Davies that he and Tom spent holidays and weekends in the country, sketching, fishing and taking photos with Tom's Kodak. Their primary roaming areas were the gentle rolling lands Tom's grandfather Tam and father John farmed, fished, and wandered in bygone days—Whitevale, Claremont, Frenchman's Bay and

HARRY B. JACKSON

Services Are Held For Harry Jackson

Services for Harry B. Jackson, 80, commercial artist, who died Tuesday in his home at 5815 Elmwood Drive, South Monroe Townsite, were at 2 p.m. today in the Allore and Holcomb funeral home. The Rev. A. D. Klontz, D.D., of St. Paul's Methodist Church officiated and burial was in Roselawn Memorial Park Cemetery.

Bearers were William Schoell, Erwin Everett, Jack Garrison, John Sisco jr., C. A. McInnis and Helmuth Thoms.

Mr. Jackson had been well known in Monroe for years for his art work in pen and ink drawings, pencil sketches, oil paintings and portrait work. MEN 5/7/53

Top Left: *Outside a Camp near Bisco,* photo, AO-DBS, 1-273-1-0-50-12.

Far Right: "Services Are Held For Harry Jackson", *Monroe Evening News,* July 5, 1953.

Bottom: *Mowat Lodge,* APMA 186.

Scarborough Bluffs. Two or three times, they went further afield to Lake Scugog. Grip Limited co-worker Tom H. Marten[xciii] took a photo of Tom gazing over a mirror-like Lake Scugog—canoes nearby.

Tom Thomson at Lake Scugog, 1910 photographed by T. H. Marten, Collection of the Tom Thomson Art Gallery, Owen Sound, gift of Margaret Murch.

Historian Ottelyn Addison claimed, in *Tom Thomson: The Algonquin Years*, that Tom took Harry to his parents' home in Owen Sound. Tom painted; Harry sketched. According to his obituary, Harry Jackson returned from trips with sketches he made of the places visited; he especially liked unusual scenes and trees.[xciv]

In May 1912, as trout lilies and bloodroot pushed through the sodden earth, Tom and Harry set off for their biggest adventure yet. Grip Limited co-worker Tom McLean, a great outdoorsman and an early visitor to Algonquin Park, had told the pair about, "… the beauty and fine fishing in that region and Tom and I thought we would try it." He also gave them a letter of introduction for Algonquin Park Superintendent George W. Bartlett. Letters of introduction, and visiting cards, were part of polite social interaction when Canada was young. There was an elaborate etiquette associated with writing and presenting such letters and Tom and Harry would have considered it a coup to have a letter of introduction to the Algonquin Park Superintendent.

Tom and Harry were full of anticipation as they rode the Grand Trunk Railway 220 kilometres north from Toronto. Tom had along his new painting outfit and the Dutch oven his Grip Limited pals gave him as a present.[xcv]

On May 18 Park Ranger Mark Robinson greeted them at the Canoe Lake train station and formally accepted the letter of introduction they had from Tom McLean for Superintendent Bartlett. Robinson introduced them to another ranger, Bud Callighen, whose berth was Smoke Lake, the area Robinson suggested for the two novices. Robinson also recommended they head to Camp Mowat to add provisions to the fishing, camping and painting gear they'd lugged along.

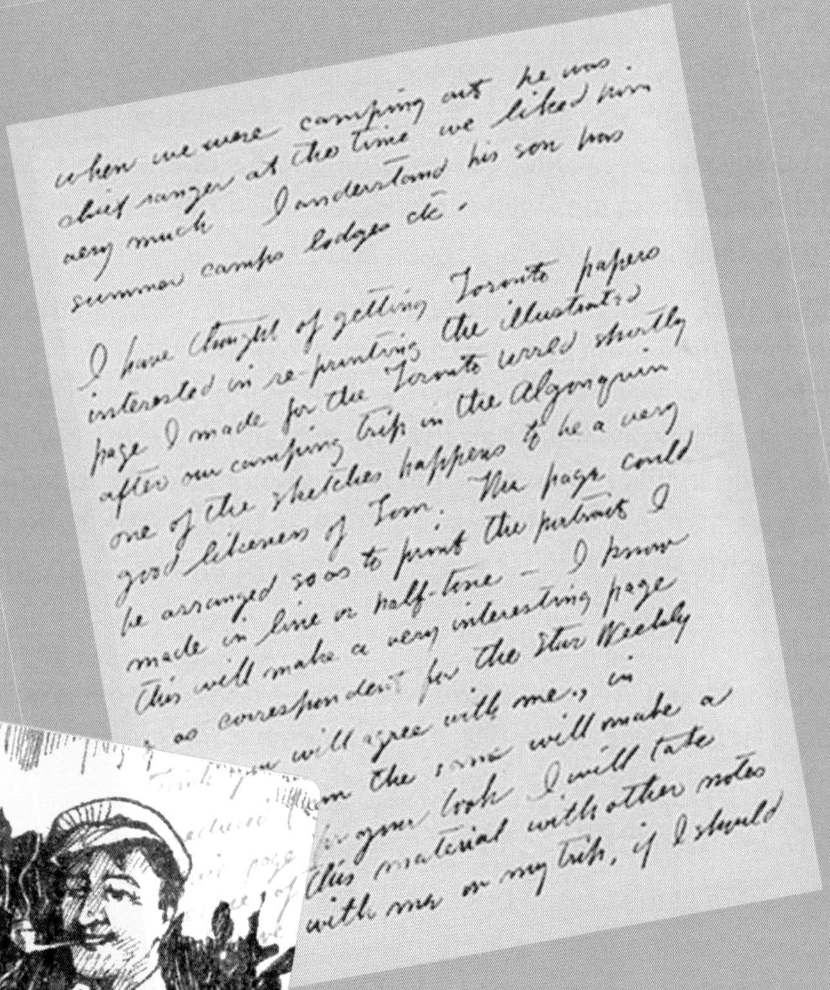

when we were camping out he was
chief ranger at the time we liked him
very much. I understand his son has
summer camps lodges etc.

I have thought of getting Toronto papers
interested in re-printing the illustrated
page I made for the Toronto World shortly
after our camping trip in the Algonquin
one of the sketches happens to be a very
good likeness of Tom. The page could
be arranged so as to print the portraits I
made in line or half-tone — I know
this will make a very interesting page
as correspondent for the Star Weekly

I think you will agree with me, in
looking them over the same will make a
on your book I will take
this material with other notes
with me on my trip, if I should

*H.B. Jackson letter, Monroe, Michigan, July 5, 1930, to
Blodwen Davies, LAC, Blodwen Davies Collection,
M.G. 30, D 38, volume 11.*

*I have thought of
getting Toronto papers
interested in reprinting
the illustrated page I
made for the "Toronto
World" shortly after
our camping trip in the
Algonquin. One of the
sketches happens to be
a very good likeness
of Tom.*

Shannon Fraser driving his wagon in front of Mowat Lodge.
Photo courtesy of Sylvia (Hayhurst) Telford, Hayhurst Point.
Annie Fraser is the first female from the right.

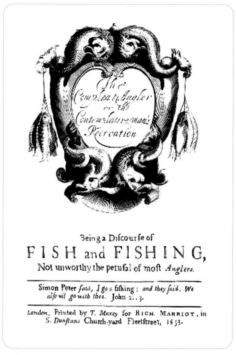

The Compleat Angler, Frontispiece, Isaac Walton, 1653, PD.

A couple named Shannon and Annie Fraser had taken over the hospital of the defunct Gilmour Lumber Company and were preparing other buildings to be Mowat Lodge.[xcvi] They were almost done with the preparations that spring and would formally open the Lodge in 1913. Tom and Harry purchased a two week food supply that included bacon, beans, rice and biscuit ingredients. Shannon Fraser watched as they loaded 60 kg of gear into their rented canoe in the teeth of a high wind. Seeing they were not experts, Fraser suggested they wait out the wind in his and Annie's Camp. Addison wrote that Thomson told Shannon Fraser, "Don't let the fellow I am with know that I am not a good canoe man or he won't go with me."[xcvii]

Indeed, Tom had little experience in a canoe as his father mistrusted them. Dad was a rowboat man. Yet, in spite of Tom's relative inexperience with the conveyance, the pair made it to the Tea Lake Dam and to Smoke Lake. In his article, Harry related that deer visited their camp every night and wolves howled in the distance. "If it was a rainy day, we would stay in camp. Tom would clean his pipes and read Walton's *Compleat Angler." Tom Thomson, Rainy Day in Camp, 1912*, painted by Harry Jackson during this trip, is in the National Gallery of Canada.

Harry's illustrations for *The Toronto Sunday World* display Tom's cooking set up: pots on a wangan hanging

97

Top Left: *Park Rangers Mark Robinson and Bud Callighen,* APMA 2906
Tom gave Callighen, *Smoke Lake, Algonquin Park,* Spring 1912, oil.

Lower Left: Tom Thomson's *camp cooking,* H.B. Jackson excerpt from
Toronto Sunday World, August 11, 1912, TRL-SC.

Top Right: "KLIM: The Producer and Her Finest Product",
Saturday Evening Post, 1920, PD.

Lower Right: *Camp Cooking set up from Camp Kitchener at O'Neill's Bay,*
photo, AO Donald B. Smith Fonds, B379123.

over the fire, a reflector oven, a long-handled frying pan. By Harry's account, the pair ate well. "Our lake trout was boiled and baked, not fried, real biscuits etc. Everything had to be cooked just so." They had a ready supply of trout, but there was also much to forage. In late May, nature offered fiddleheads, watercress and wild leeks. After they ate Harry wrote, "You chat for awhile as the day dies out and the dark creeps into the woods around. And then as that still hush of the north sifts in with the mist, and the lake glistens with the last red glows of the west, you stop talking and just think."

Tom must have been thinking that he never wanted to leave!

After two weeks of this quiet fishing idyll, Harry returned to Grip Limited. Tom stayed. He'd become expert enough with a paddle to guide two Toronto anglers, Leonard Mack and Harry Bracken. They went through Smoke, and Ragged Lakes, out of the Park to Crown Lake. As there was no hunting in the Park, Tom had to go beyond its borders to shoot small game for the Dutch oven and long-handled frying pan. With the advancing spring, Tom also added wild strawberries to his fine fare. The red treasures winked from the moist under-

growth at the edge of woods. Ottelyn Addison noted, "There were plenty of berry patches, the aftermath of lumbering or a regrowth area after forest fires."[xcviii]

Harry Jackson described Tom's sketches from that May 1912 trip as, "a few notes, skylines and color effects."[xcix] Back in new lodging at 66 Wellesley Street

Tom Thomson. *Morning Cloud,* 1913. Oil on canvas, 72 x 101.4 cm. The Thomson Collection at the Art Gallery of Ontario, Toronto. © 2017, Art Gallery of Ontario.

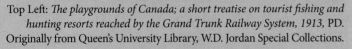
Fishing for Black Bass in the St. Lawrence

Top Left: *The playgrounds of Canada; a short treatise on tourist fishing and hunting resorts reached by the Grand Trunk Railway System, 1913,* PD. Originally from Queen's University Library, W.D. Jordan Special Collections.

Top Right: *Wild Strawberry,* photo from plantwatch.ca.

Left: *Weeds: How to forage for free super foods,* photo from littleecofootprints.com.

Lower Right: *Fishing for Black Bass in the St. Lawrence,* Louis Rhead, from *The Basses-Freshwater and Marine, William C. Harris, 1905,* PD.

that winter, Tom transformed the notes to which Harry referred. They became finished works with dazzling sky effects. Tom's passionate affair with Algonquin Park had begun.

After this wondrous northern experience, Harry, who was by then 41-years-old, returned to Cambridge, Massachusetts to marry his sweetheart Mabelle Zoller. In 1916, the couple settled in Monroe, Michigan, where Harry worked and headed the art department of the Consolidated Paper Company for the next 24 years. He designed packages for national product campaigns. He and Mabelle led a quiet life.

Harry was much saddened when he heard of Tom's untimely death. He was even more devastated when Mabelle died in 1939. They had just completed their dream home in South Monroe Township. He retired the next year, occasionally working on freelance art projects at the desk a friend provided at the Monroe Engraving and Design Co.

In all those years, Harry Jackson never forgot his time in Algonquin Park with Tom Thomson. He told Davies, "I look back on that trip as one of my best vacations."

Harry Jackson died alone in this home May 5, 1953.

The Food Connection

Tom's partial provision list for two weeks with Harry Jackson in May 1912 included bacon, beans, rice and biscuit ingredients. On his second trip with William Smithson Broadhead in late summer and fall of 1912, the provision list for two months included flour, sugar, pork, beans, rice, prunes, desiccated potatoes, onions and milk. In a May 8, 1917, letter to Dr. MacCallum, Tom describes the items he had, and would get, for a two week trip with Dr. MacCallum and Curtis Williamson. The list included, "one gallon of maple syrup, a pail of jam, plenty bacon, potatoes, bread, tea, sugar, all kinds of canned stuff …" He also tried, but failed, to get some chocolate, coffee and Klim (a dried milk brand he was said to use in large amounts).

These partial provision lists provide insight into Tom's cooking and baking habits on the trail. And although Tom left no recipes, he left lots for the imagination. What could he have made with the listed ingredients? What did he forage and cook? Period cook books supply recipes that were *de jour* when Canada was young.

Top Left: *Scarborough Bluffs,* Tom Thomson, photo, *Bulletin 16 #2.*

Top Right: *Tom Thomson Fishing at Tea Lake Dam,* photo, LAC, PA-187135.

Lower Left: *Shannon Fraser picking up people from the station* Sylvia (Hayhurst) Telford photo Tom Thomson sitting in the wagon at front. Shannon Fraser bottom right corner.

Lower Right: *Canoe Lake train station,* APMA 28.

There is a recipe that won a prize in a contest held by the Department of Marine and Fisheries in Ottawa in 1921, in *Eat More Fish: recipes and hints for the cook*. This is a nice and easy recipe that one can easily imagine Tom using.

Pan Broiled Pickerel

"Clean well and wash fish thoroughly. Dry with a clean white cloth. Have dripping and a little butter or butter alone, if it can be afforded, well heated in a frying pan. Dip pieces in milk, sprinkle with salt and pepper, then roll in flour, hastily roll it in bread crumbs. Put in grease to fry to a golden brown, serve hot."

The Home cook book / compiled by ladies of Toronto and chief cities and towns in Canada and published in 1923 by Hunter–Rose Co. in Toronto, has a recipe for bass. Shad, pickerel and trout may all be made in the same way.

Mrs. P.B. Ayer's Baked Black Bass

"Eight good-sized onions chopped fine; half that quantity of bread crumbs, butter size of a hen's egg, plenty of pepper and salt, mix thoroughly with anchovy sauce until quite red.

Stuff your fish with the compound and pour the rest over, previously sprinkling it with a little red pepper. Shad, pickerel and trout are good the same way."

Mrs. Ayer advises that tomatoes may be used instead of anchovies, as they are more economical. "If using them, take pork in place of butter and chop fine."

With fish aplenty and provision lists heavy on carbohydrates, I pondered the question of vegetables. There was always plenty to forage, depending upon the season. *Canoe and Camp Cookery: A Practical Cook Book for Canoeists, Corinthian Sailors and Outers*,[1] which was originally published by Seneca in 1885, provides an overview:

Greens

"When in camp or on a cruise, a most delicious dish can be made of boiled greens, of which a large variety of weeds and plants furnishes the material. Dandelion leaves, nettles, milkweed, spinach, young beet tops, turnip tops, mustard, narrow dock, mountain cow-slip, kale cabbage, poke, sprouts and other "weeds" are good. They should be picked over carefully, washed in three or four waters, and soaked in cold

---

[1] "Corinthian Sailor: of or pertaining to an amateur sailor or yachtsman", *Webster's*, 1913.

water half an hour; then drain and put in enough boiling salt water to cover them. Press them down till the pot is full, as they "boil away" and lose more than half in substance. Cover, and boil steadily till tender. Then drain and press out the water. Season to taste with butter, pepper and salt. Greens are good boiled with salt pork, bacon, corned beef or ham."

In Miss E. Warner's *Purity Flour Cook Book,* published by the Domestic Science Department of the MacDonald Institute in 1917, on page 124 we find a recipe to go with Tom's fresh fish catch.

Dandelions

"Gather only the freshly grown plants; best when the dew is on them. The tenderest leaves make an excellent salad with bacon dressing. The whole plant, after thoroughly washing, may be boiled until tender, drained, chopped fine, seasoned with salt, vinegar and a liberal measure of butter. Those who think it too bitter may use half spinach or beet leaves or sorrel, in which case the dandelion should be partly cooked before the more succulent plant is added. It cannot be too well recommended."

Miss Warner also recommends:

Mushrooms

"Gather them fresh, pare and cut off the stems, dip them in melted butter, season with salt and pepper, broil them on both sides over a clear fire. Serve on toast."

Before we picture Tom and Harry savouring a meal at Tea Lake in 1912, it's time to make bannock. Page 285 of *The Home Cook Book* has a recipe by someone identified simply as "M".

Bannocks

"One pint corn meal, pour on it boiling water to thoroughly wet it. Let it stand a few minutes; add salt and one egg and a little sweet cream, or a tablespoon of melted butter. Make into balls and fry in hot lard."

The Klim Cookbook also has a recipe:

Bannock

"I cup flour, 1 teaspoon baking powder, 1 tablespoon Klim, 1 pinch salt, ½ tablespoon lard or bacon grease

Rub shortening into dry ingredients, then add enough water to give a firm dough. Place in a well-greased pan and bake slowly over hot coals until a straw inserted in the middle comes away clean. For sweet bannock, add a little sugar and some raisins. Be sure to bake slowly—slow cooking makes good bannock."

Ready to eat with Tom and Harry?

Pull on up to the campfire. The bass is baking in the reflector oven. Tom is just now draining the salt pork water from the dandelion greens. He's going to mash them with butter and sprinkle them with bacon bits he rescued from the morning's pan drippings. Earlier he'd mixed up dough; Harry is tending the bannocks baking in the long-handled frying pan.

The few morel mushrooms they foraged sit skewered on thin green sticks, ready to be roasted at the last minute. The water for tea steams in the kettle hanging on the wangan. Tom's pipe smoke hangs in the cool evening air as he bends to test the readiness of the bass. The metal plates sit nearby with precut pieces of toasted bread—bread Tom baked yesterday in the Dutch oven. Come and get it!

"Vic Aures Crane", illustration from *Wildwood Wisdom*, Ellsworth Jaeger, plate 90, p 203. Courtesy of Keith Thornborrow.

Top Left: *William "Bill" Smithson Broadhead 1911.*
Probably at 119 Summerhill Avenue, Toronto. Arthur Lismer
Collection. Purchased with the assistance of a Movable Cultural
Property grant accorded by the Department of Canadian Heritage
under the terms of the Cultural Property Export and Import Act, and
with the generous support of the McMichael Canadian Art
Foundation. McMichael Canadian. Art Collection Archives. ALC-
Photo Album.2.p.16,no.4.

Top Right: *Mrs. Legace's Boarding House pre-1913 fire in
Biscotasing,* photo, AO-DBS, 1-273-1-0-19-10.

Lower Right: "Illustration of his room at 119 Summerhill",
William Smithson Broadhead letter to Ivy and Tom, May 22, 1910, SA, LD1980-13 p1.jpeg.

CHAPTER TEN

William Smithson Broadhead, the Figure Man

"There is one thing I can knock them silly at, and that is drawing the figure. I have the whole bunch beat." W.S. Broadhead, letter to his father, December 11, 1910

William Broadhead arrived in Toronto in the winter of 1910. The award-winning Sheffield School of Art graduate was 22-years-old. He found lodgings at 119 Summerhill Avenue with the Logier family who treated him like a son. The gregarious young man quickly made friends and availed himself of winter sports that included skating and wind sailing on Toronto Bay[c]. The fine work he did at the Rolph and Clark Lithographic Co.[ci], and his freelance assignments for *The Courier* newspaper, brought him to the attention of Albert Robson, Art Director at Grip Limited. Robson hired the confident Yorkshire man.

William wrote to his father about Grip Limited on December 10, 1910: "They are a much more refined and cultured set of fellows …. There is no chewing, spitting or cursing here. Their conversation is clean and interesting and they all seem so very ambitious." William was out sketching with his new workmates, shooting ducks at Scarborough Bluffs[1] and working his way into Toronto's art world soon after starting at Grip Limited.

Albert Robson invited him to the Arts and Letters Club; he bantered about Canadian art with John Beatty at the Graphic Arts Club; he prepared entries for the Ontario Society of Artists show at the C.N.E. He even boasted to his parents he'd soon be an Associate of the Royal Canadian Academy telling them, "I could knock shots off half the so-called big guns here." His letters home paint a picture of confidence.

[1]Arthur Lismer, *Pull the String Tommy, 1911,* cartoon, pokes fun at Tom Thomson as a duck hunter.

The young man had another goal. He kept hearing about wondrous Algonquin Park. Everyone at Grip Limited said it was painters' country. Early on he'd been to Robson's home where, "the boss showed me hundreds of fine photographs of the north country." When Harry Jackson returned to the Grip Limited art room in the summer of 1912, his tales further whetted William's desire for adventure. The voices all said, "Go north, young man!"

William invited Tom to room at the Logiers' when he came back from his very first Algonquin Park adventure that summer. There in their shared room he plumped for another area Tom McLean had recommended for fishing, hunting and painting. Algoma was a wild, isolated, northern area teeming with fish, wildlife—and risk. William was a keen hunter and risk, a must.

The pair departed after the worst of the bug season at the end of July 1912. The only boarding house in Biscotasing (Bisco) was Matilda Legace's square-timbered, slate-coloured, two-storey establishment. Mrs. Legace had the sole eatery for strangers. If you were smartly dressed you were allowed to sit at a table for four; otherwise you shared the fare at a table with 14 hungry men. Tom and William sat at the long table.

One of the most beautiful women in town was the young Métis woman, Marie Girard. For a few weeks that summer, Marie was constantly before young William's eyes. Mrs. Legace had her assist in the dining room[cii], as well as assigning her maid duties for the nine rooms she had for guests. Judging by the fact that only 270 people called Bisco home in 1912, the beautiful Marie was in all likelihood, the woman with whom William fell deeply in love, the one about whom he wrote his parents from New York City, on August. 5, 1913: "I don't know whether I told you before, but the little half breed girl I met last summer in Bisco was the only girl who has ever stolen my affections for any time." Later in the same letter William added, "I poisoned the affections with common sense and reason."

Who knows what part Tom Thomson played in cooling William's ardour? Tom was 11 years older than William. He'd had his heart broken by a younger woman in Seattle. He'd have had a few words of common sense, and reasons for not taking up with Marie. Fortunately, preparations for the lengthy trip diverted them.

Rangers in Canoes photo, AO-DBS, 1-273-0-1-25-5.

Welcoming the Duke of Connaught to Bisco, 1912. Extreme left standing, Ferg Legace. Photo, AO-DBS, 1-273-1-0-18-13.

The Hudson's Bay Company store had an authoritative factor[ciii] who ruled the town. Harry Woodworth oversaw the purchase of Tom and William's two month supply of flour, sugar, pork, beans, rice, prunes, baking powder, desiccated potatoes, onions and milk. According to a September 27, 1912, *Owen Sound Sun*[civ] article, along with sketching and camping outfits, each man had approximately 200 pounds (90 kg) of supplies. A photo of Tom from around this time shows a heavily laden Peterborough canoe with dunnage stowed.

At the beginning of August, Tom and William left love behind and voyaged from Bisco Lake to Ramsay Lake and then through Mississagi, Green and Clear Lakes with all the rivers and portages in between. At Green Lake, a cloudburst swamped their canoe; they tipped into the water, but salvaged everything. They were living the wild life.

For meals, they supplemented provisions with partridge, fish, forest greens and berries. Tom knew where to look for chanterelles, wild grape leaves and raspberries. William hunted. Nature was a bounteous larder. Tom told his brother-in-law James Henry shortly after the trip, "I've picked raspberries on one side of a log, while a big black bear picked berries on the other side."[cv]

For days they paddled, painted, photographed, portaged, camped and cooked. They had close encounters with hulking moose and howling wolves. Tom described an arm's length meeting he had in the underbrush, a story his sister Louisa retold in a 1931 letter to Blodwen Davies: "It was a large timber wolf, one of the largest he had ever seen, its head, neck and breast were jet black and the body the usual grey color. He said it was the most beautiful animal he had ever seen."

Top Left: *On the Forty Mile Rapids,* photo, AO-DBS, 1-273-1-0-52-2.

Top Right: *Couple Walking on a Snow Flurry,* William Smithson Broadhead, oil, johnmoran.com.

Lower Left: *Camp site with fire,* photo taken by Archie Belaney, AO-DBS, 1-273-1-0-50-15.

Lower Right: *Aubrey Falls,* photo, AO-DBS, 1-273-1-0-50-2.

Tom and William entered the Mississagi Forest Reserve in late August. Having crossed the height of land dividing the Spanish and Mississagi watersheds, canoeing was easier. Tom wrote to his friend John McRuer that the weather, painting, and fishing weren't great (mostly pike),[cvi] but he and William were making the best of it. William provided meat for the pot, and Tom searched for oyster mushrooms, sumac and wild ginger. Tom would have used his creativity to shape the meals that nature and their talents provided.

By the time they reached Aubrey Falls, Tom and William had done nearly 200 km and more than 20 portages, mostly in poor weather; they still had many kilometres to go. At the Forty Mile Rapids, the fishing party of Colonel Mason[cvii] and his two nephews came upon the pair salvaging sketches that had dumped into the roiling waters. A great many rolls of film were gone; others were damaged. When they made it to Squaw Chute, a settler drove them to Bruce Mines. They arrived in Owen Sound via Midland on September 26, 1912. They were bronzed and full of themselves as outdoorsmen.

Tom's boss Albert Robson described Tom's return to work: "Strolling up from the station in his woodsman outfit and carrying the bundles of sketches, he reported his return to work and left the sketches for inspection. We urged him to paint one of his sketches upon a large canvas, and gave him the keys and use of the studio on weekends. So *A Northern Lake* came into being in 1913, his first attempt on a large canvas."[cviii]

Ironically, William had too good a time with Tom. Fearing he'd become overly enthralled with shooting and fishing, he decamped to New York at the end of 1912. He worked as an illustrator for the satirical *Judge* magazine before joining King Edward's Horse (The King's Overseas Dominion Regiment), a cavalry unit during World War I.

Hoofprints over America, book cover, William Smithson Broadhead.

Tom would have been amused that later in life his young friend ended up as a British–American animal and sports painter, who wrote *Hoof Prints Over America* in 1951. William's career included a portrait of Elizabeth Taylor on the horse she rode in *National Velvet.* Broadhead had a full adventurous life but his good times with Tom Thomson were over in 1912.

Above: *Northern Lake,* Winter, 1912–1913, Tom Thomson, oil on canvas, 71.1x102.4 cm. Gift of the Government of the Province of Ontario, 1972. c 2017 Art Gallery of Ontario. This is the first painting that was bought by the Ontario Government.

Left: *Harry Woodworth, Hudson Bay Factor, Bisco,* photo, AO 1-273-1-0-24-1.

Lower Right: *Ice Fishing Toronto Island,* CTA, Fonds 1244, f1244_it0445.

The Food Connection

Tom and William undertook a long, difficult canoe trip that included camps of a few days' duration so that they could hunt, fish and forage. In a letter to John McRuer, Tom complained that it was cold and wet, and that the pike was way too plentiful. He told his brothers-in-law about picking berries. William would have hunted water-fowl and small forest animals. Nature's harvest in August and September included chanterelles and blueberries.

I started my search for menu items that Tom and William might have used by reading Izaak Walton's *Compleat Angler.* Harry Jackson had said Tom regularly read it and it was a great starting point. The pair had an over-abundance of pike on their trip and Walton's book from 1653 had a secret recipe for roasting gutted pike. Here is Walton's 17th century roasted pike:

Roasted Pike

"The pike's liver is shredded with thyme, sweet marjoram and a little winter savory; to these put some pickled oysters, and some anchovies, two or three, both these last whole; to these you must add also a pound of sweet butter, which you are to mix with the herbs that are shred, and let them all be well salted …. These being thus mixed with a blade or two of mace, must be put into the pike's belly, and then his belly so sewed up as to keep all the butter in his belly … but take not off the scales: then you are to thrust the spit through his mouth out at his tail; and then take four, or five, or six split sticks … and a convenient quantity of tape or filleting; these laths are to be tied round about the pike's body from his head to his tail, and the tape tied somewhat thick to prevent his breaking or falling off from the spit: let him be roasted very leisurely, and often basted with claret wine and anchovies and butter mixed together, and also with what moisture falls from him into the pan; when you have roasted him sufficiently, you are to hold under him … such a dish as you purpose to eat him out of; and let him fall into it with the sauce that is roasted in his belly; and by this means the pike will be kept unbroken and complete."

113

Tom would simply not have the requisite items in Walton's recipe above, but I had no doubt he was inspired by it. What might he have had along or have available to forage? What were his substitutes? He'd have had the pike's liver, butter, salt pork, winter savory found in wetlands, and whatever dried herbs he had along from his father's garden.

I left the matter of the pike there, as Harry Jackson had also said Tom boiled fish. I found a 19th century recipe for boiled fish in *Canoe and Camp Cookery*. It was positively Spartan by comparison to Walton's pike but much more doable.

Boiled Fish

"Tie or pin the fish (which should not weigh less than three pounds) in a clean cloth. If the pot is too small for the fish, skewer the tail into the mouth. Put into enough boiling water to cover it about an inch, and simmer steadily until done …. If a couple of tablespoonfuls of salt and four ditto of vinegar are put into the water the fish will cook sooner. About twenty-five minutes are necessary for a three-pound fish, and over that, six minutes extra to every pound. An underdone fish is not fit to eat, and one boiled too long is insipid. When the meat separates easily from the backbone it is cooked just right. Take it up, remove the cloth carefully, and pour over it the following:

Fish Sauce

Put two tablespoonfuls of butter and two ditto of flour into a hot frying pan over the fire and mix them together with a spoon into a smooth paste. Pour over very gradually about a pint of the water in which the fish was boiled, stirring it well. Boil up once and season with pepper and salt."

After that recipe, consider the pike boiled. And now, what better way to serve it than with desiccated potatoes and powdered milk brought to creamy life with pristine lake water and herbed butter? Maybe Tom and William found chanterelle mushrooms, which Tom fried and folded into the potatoes.

For dessert it's blueberries. Tom was known to bake a mean blueberry pie. Ottelyn Addison and Elizabeth Harwood said in *Tom Thomson: The Algonquin Years* that, "A reflector oven was standard equipment on a canoe trip. If Thomson stayed in camp a day or two, he might make a blueberry pie or some biscuits."

In reminiscences of Tom, William Little wrote: "Tom had picked some blueberries and was making a pie, which he baked in his reflector over the campfire. Tom said he did not know how the pie would come out, but if they could not eat the crust, at least they could eat the berries."So, it's blueberry pie on their menu for sure.

Over the days in their transit camp, Tom and William would probably have had the ducks to roast that William shot. While Tom baked, William plucked feathers.

Mrs. Beeton's Cookery Book published in 1912 by Ward, Lock & Co., London, has standard recipes on pages 189–190 for Duck, Stewed with Green Peas; Ducks, Roasted; Fowl, Boiled; Fowl, Brown Fricassee of[1]; Fowl Curried, Fowl Galantine of; Fowl, Hashed and Fowl, Ragout of.

Ducks, Roasted

"Ingredients: 2 ducks, sage and onion stuffing … $\frac{1}{2}$ pint of stock, $\frac{1}{2}$ oz. of flour, salt and pepper, apple sauce.

Method: Stuff the body of the ducks with the onion farce or stuffing, and truss them as directed. Baste them well with hot fat, and roast them in front of a clear fire, or in a moderately hot oven, for about 1 hour, basting frequently. When done, pour off the fat, and if a thick gravy is preferred, brown the flour in the dripping-pan before adding the stock. Bring the gravy to boiling point, season to taste, simmer for 1 or 2 minutes, and serve in a sauceboat."

For Tom and Broadhead's late summer trip, the menu is wide open for the imagination.

---

[1]*of = fricassee galantine and ragout of fowl*

A Ranger in the Doorway of a Shelter-Hut. Photograph by Tom Thomson. c. 1912. Library and Archives Canada. Photo.

Left: *Archie with Fish,* photo, before WWI, AO-DBS, 1-273-1-0-1-46-23.

Top: *Archie Belaney with short hair after WWI,* photo, AO-DBS, 1-273-1-0-1-46-4.

Bottom: *Archie with Braids,* photo, AO-DBS, 1-273-1-0-1-45-1.

From Archie to Grey Owl

Left: *Grey Owl, (Archibald Belaney),* Yousuf Karsh photo, LAC-1664228 Mikan ID 3192426.

Right: *Archie Belaney in Bisco,* left to right, Jimmy Sanders, Donat Legace, Archie Belaney, Raphael Legace, Marie Woodworth, 1912, photo, AO-DBS, 1-273-1-0-46-2.

CHAPTER ELEVEN

The Bromance,[1] Tom Thomson and Archie Belaney/Grey Owl

"With his books on Indians, his menagerie, and his solitary walks to look for plants and animals, the lonely boy lived in a dream world of his own making. Creatively, he invented two fictional parents. To explain their absence he developed the story further, later stating that his father was a western plainsman and his mother a Native American. So began the fabulous story of his origins that he would elaborate and refine for the remainder of his life." Archibald Stansfeld Belaney *Dictionary of Canadian Biography*

Archie Belaney, the imaginative British lad born in Hastings in 1888, took many years to assume the native Canadian identity of Grey Owl. When his transition was complete, he was so convincing as a First Nations author, speaker and conservationist that he managed a private audience with King George VI of England. Princess Elizabeth, the current queen, was part of the Royal Command Performance at Buckingham Palace on December 10, 1937.[cix] Long before that royal meeting, Tom Thomson met Canada's notorious trickster.

In the summer of 1912, Tom Thomson, William Smithson Broadhead and Archie Belaney were on a collision course. At that point, young Archie had squeezed a great deal of living into his six years in Canada. From his entry into Canada at Halifax on April 6, 1906 he'd made his way to Toronto, earned his train fare to Cobalt by working in the men's wear department at the T. Eaton Company[cx] and had gotten off the train in Temiskaming. There he lived with the fur trading Guppy family and picked up outdoorsmen's skills.[cxi] Guppy's granddaughter Joan Luttrell relates, "It was Grandpa who first set Archie up with a

[1]*bromance: a close but non-sexual relationships between two men, Oxford Dictionaries online*

Fire Rangers' Hall at Bear Lake, photo, AO-DBS, 273-1-0-43-12.
Archie married Angele Egwuna of the Teme-Augama Anishnabai community there on August 23, 1910.

Archie had already practiced in childhood play in Hastings. Next Archie lived with the Ojibwa people of Bear Island who further honed his hunting and trapping skills. He became deeply tanned and married an Ojibwa woman named Angele Egwuna (1888–1955).[cxiii]

In May 1912, Archie left Angele and his new baby Agnes to search for a life unfettered by family responsibilities. He headed to Bisco to see if he'd succeed in signing up as a fire ranger. Chief Fire Ranger Frank Duval hired 50 men each summer for the Mississagi Forest Reserve. The rangers patrolled by canoe, had a few fire towers as lookouts and had a cabin at Bark Lake where the Mississagi River drained into it.

woodsmen's 'kit' and gave him his first trap line to work. Grandpa, who made him his first snowshoes, taught him how to handle a canoe, shoot the rapids, read the trail, and most important to Archie, it was Grandpa who gave him his first knowledge of native religion and customs and taught him his first Indian words."[cxii] Joan adds that her Uncles Gordon and Clifford Guppy taught Archie how to throw a tomahawk and hunting knife with pinpoint accuracy—skills

Archibald "Grey Owl" Belaney, Arthur Lismer drawing, Arts and Letters Club Archive courtesy of Scott James.

While Archie waited for the fire ranger selection that May, he stayed at Matilda Legace's boarding house in Bisco. There in the parlour, the tall, bronzed man with native ways, played piano and recited his favourite British verse. No one paid that contradiction any mind.[cxiv]

Matilda's son Ferg Legace was only 12-years-old that spring. He remembered that Archie played gramophone records over and over until he had them by heart and could play them on the parlour piano. The tall stranger also played the piano for local dances.[cxv]

Marie Girard, a beautiful, Métis, boarding house maid entered this scene. (Picture her with an armful of fresh linens.) She spotted the lively young man who looked a great deal like her Algonquin relatives. Marie fell hard for Archibald Belaney. It didn't matter to her that he was married. Unfortunately for Marie, Archie had no time for romance—not then. He got the ranger job and headed to his ranger duties at the end of June. A month later, Marie met William Smithson Broadhead, who fell hard for her. A strange love triangle!

Tom and William followed Archie's route that summer when they canoed from Bisco to Bark Lake. The trio met on the trail by the sheerest of serendipity.[cxvi] One of Tom's water-damaged photos shows two men at a campfire; the third person has to be the photographer, Tom. The photo is hard to make out, but when blown up, the man with suspenders appears to be William Broadhead and the other man wearing a vest and with long hair, is in all likelihood, Archie.

Canoeists' Camp. Photograph by Tom Thomson. c. 1912.
Library and Archives Canada. Photo: NGC

It's a good guess that Marie Girard did not come into the conversation when 35-year-old Tom sat by the campfire with the two "youngsters" from Britain,[cxvii]

121

both a decade younger than he. It's a good guess because Archie was known to be short-tempered and had that hunting knife at the ready and William was a blusterer. It would not have sat well with either man that within the period of a month they had both romanced the same beautiful Métis woman.

If Marie Girard did not come up in the campfire talk, fire ranging must have. It can't be coincidence that both Tom and Archie ended up as fire rangers in the Mattagami[1] area for at least part of the summer of 1913. They'd likely discussed the possibilities of sharing the experience, and why shouldn't they? Archie and Tom had much in common. Newspaper columnist Doug Mackey compares Archie and Tom.[cxviii] Mackey starts his comparisons with broad statements, such as, "Both men were similarly independent, itinerant and iconoclastic …" and "Both men loved the woods, canoeing and fishing," and then he provides examples that make it easy to see how their natures and activities were similar. Tom and Archie would really have liked one another.

Another Belaney biographer, Jane Billinghurst, claims that in the winter of 1912, Archie traveled south from Bisco to Toronto and Montreal, returning the following summer.[cxix] If Billinghurst is accurate, Archie and Tom

had further opportunity to discuss plans for Mattagami. Did they?

The best fuel to fire the Thomson–Belaney bromance theory is the huge gap in both their chronologies for the summer of 1913. Tom Thomson authorities supply no sound whereabouts for him from January to fall of 1913. They merely state Tom, **may** work as a fire ranger on the Mattagami Reserve where his name appears on the 1913 pay list. Archie Belaney scholars[cxx] are likewise vague about his whereabouts that summer. Were Tom and Archie off the radar in 1913 for some quiet months together in a remote area between Sudbury and Timmins?

In an article titled, "Knew Famous Tom Thomson as Good Doughnut Maker" in the Owen Sound *Sun Times*[cxxi] Belaney told art critic William Arthur Deacon that many fire rangers met at the ranger cabin at Lake Minisinakwa in Gogoma. Archie admits that one of the fire rangers he met was Tom Thomson, a painter and great doughnut maker. Since Tom wasn't a fire ranger at Lake Minisinakwa in 1912, Archie's comments refer to the summer of 1913—and being with Tom. In the Toronto *Mail and Empire* article of November 9, 1936 ("Famed Canvases Found in Cabin") from which the Owen Sound doughnut article derived, Tom's boss

[1] *Mattagami is also referred to as Metagami.*

remembered Tom's time as a fire ranger on Lake Minisinakwa. Mattagami craftsman, William Moore (1889–1974), told generations of youngsters that Tom Thomson lived in the forestry building on the treeless point of land overlooking Lake Mattagami when he was a fire ranger in "these parts."[cxxii]

Above: *William Moore, Ojibway craftsman of Mattagami Reserve near Gogoma, working on a birchbark basket, 1957, photo John Macfie, Mattagami, AO, C 330-13-0-0-110.*

Archie, Robson and William Moore place Tom in Mattagami in 1913—the former two mention Lake Minisinakwa and the latter locates him at Lake Mattagami. If Tom did indeed meet up with Archie at Lake Minisinakwa, perhaps they headed to points further north? The Tom Thomson image of the mystery ranger in the doorway shows an Archie look-alike. The tall, lanky man dressed in a vest and standing in the doorway of a ranger cabin is similar to other Archie Belaney photos. Did Tom accidentally run into Archie or did they plan a meeting for the summer of 1913? **And, if the look-alike isn't Archie, with whom else was Tom in the woods that summer?**

Tom and Archie's locations become clearer in the fall of 1913. Joan Murray says Tom met park ranger Tom Wattie near South River. Biographer, Donald B. Smith, says Archie guided Toronto businessman Frank Coryell on a 10 day fishing expedition after the end of the fire ranger season. Smith has Archie heading south after that expedition. He visits with Frank Coryell, then the manager of Bedell Furnishings in Toronto, in the winter of 1913.[cxxiii]

Archie looked up Tom while in Toronto. He remembered that Tom was associated with a graphic arts firm. A Grip Limited employee redirected Archie to former art director Albert Robson who had gone to Rous and Mann. Robson offered to phone around to help Archie locate his "fire ranger friend". Tom had moved that year—from Isabella Street to Wellesley. He was hard to locate. When the two men finally connected, Tom took Archie to an arts club. Archie called it "the Artists' Club".

In November 1936, when Archie had totally assumed his Grey Owl identity, Albert Robson sat in on the aforementioned interview conducted by William Arthur Deacon. It was a tricky encounter for which Archie required fancy footwork. Robson knew that the man seated before him, dressed and acting the part

Right: *Cave and Basin*, photo, Byron Harmon, Whyte Museum v263-5958. This photo appears to show Tom Thomson in the Banff area. His chronology makes the most likely date for such a visit, late spring or summer 1913. The person to his left in the pool bears strong similarities to Archie Belaney.

Mountain Thomson, oil, said to be painted by Tom Thomson, owned by D. Hay.

of the First Nations environmentalist Grey Owl, was in fact Archie Belaney. He'd met him when he'd helped him find Tom in 1913. He recognized him and said so, "You came down from the north more than 20 years ago, and got me to do some phoning for you to locate Tom Thomson." (Oh, no, Archie must have thought, I wasn't Grey Owl at that point 20 years ago. What now?)

Grey Owl engaged in obfuscation. He claimed he didn't know Tom was an artist back when he met him in Mattagami: "I go more by faces than names and never connected the man who made the doughnuts with the famous painter."[cxxiv] The lies Grey Owl piled on became more obvious to Robson when Archie admitted he had three works by Tom Thomson on the walls of Beaver Lodge on Ajawaan Lake in Saskatchewan. Robson knew Grey Owl was a fraud; he chose not to expose him.

The theory of Tom and Archie together in 1913 doesn't end there. It's made more complicated by the recent discovery of a painting said to be by Tom Thomson showing mountains.[cxxv] The currently accepted Thomson canon places him near mountains only in Seattle at the beginning of the 20th century when he's inexperienced with oils.

Interestingly, a photo by Canadian alpine photographer Byron Harmon, provides a reasonable explanation for later Thomson paintings of mountains. Harmon's photo of the Hot Springs at the Cave and Basin pool in Banff National Park, shows two men side by side in the water. The one is very similar to Tom and the other could be Archie. Was there an escapade to the Rockies?

If Archie and Tom did go west for a brief spell, the summer of 1913 is the best fit. The Byron Harmon photo shows leaves on the trees by the bath house pool, thus limiting the time period to late spring or summer. Early Thomson biographer Blodwen Davies notes that Tom frequently took time off from painting during the summers: "He was not keen about painting greens."[cxxvi] Train schedules from that period indicate that trains west could be boarded at Bisco. And, other than the comments already discussed, that both men were in Mattagami, there's nothing to contradict the idea that Tom and Archie left for a short time to go to Banff and environs—on the QT.

Archie would have felt the QT necessary—and not for reasons modern readers might suspect. Neither Archie nor Tom need have worried about the snickers associated with a bromance. Back then, outdoorsmen routinely went on hunting and fishing expeditions for extended periods of time; they still do. In 1912 Tom and William Broadhead ran into the Hayes Fishing Party out on a long outing in the woods. To emphasize the matter further, Tom spoke to a reporter after his and William's trip down the Mississagi River. No secrets there! ("Local Man's Experience in Northern Wilds", Owen Sound, *Sun Times*, September 27, 1912)

Archie had a different reason to hide a trip west. He was pupating. By 1913 he was almost totally in his new form—set to shed his British past. Grey Owl would emerge (and but for WWI probably would have). This Grey Owl couldn't leave evidence of a person called, Archie Belaney, going west with Tom Thomson, the painter who had just sold *A Northern Lake* to the Ontario government for $250. That could trap him in his old identity—maybe even make his transition impossible. Any trip to the Rockies had to be quiet and without traces. Tom and Archie had time, funds and reasons for secrecy. Did Tom Thomson and Archie Belaney go west in 1913?

The answer to this question is open to discussion, as are Tom's whereabouts in the summer of 1913. What is known is that Archie wasn't the only one in transition at that point. Tom was in the position to ponder his transformation into a full-time artist with the small fortune from the sale of *A Northern Lake*, and the offer of Dr. MacCallum's economic support for a year.

Tom and Archie's talks in 1913 provide interesting food for thought—even if further research debunks the idea the talks took place. They could have ranged over topics such as art, nature, animal conservation, identity, and their futures. Both men were growing into new senses of self—deciding who they wanted to be. Who knows if days and nights of conversation between like-minded men helped that process?

If Tom did 'meet' Grey Owl, it was during Archie's rehearsals for the role. Tom missed the full theatrical production. Tom and Archie had commitments in 1914. While Tom was a guide and Algonquin Park mentor in 1914, Archie again spent the season as a fire ranger. Archie partnered with Bob Wilson for two months during which time the lad complained that Archie's touch with salt was too heavy on the bannock. Then he paddled along the Goulais River with ranger Bill Draper. That winter, Archie resumed the relationship he'd started with Marie Girard the preceding year. After the season of trapping, he left and Marie was pregnant. She died of tuberculosis shortly after giving birth to a lad who became known as Johnny Gero.

Johnny Gero, 1939 before WWII, photo, AO-DBS, 273-1-0-11-25.

Tom and Archie never saw one another again but Tom did send Archie three paintings before the latter went to war in May 1915—perhaps, pictures of mountains? Albert Robson had tipped Archie to the value of his three paintings in 1936. Perhaps, he no longer felt they were safe on the walls of Beaver Lodge—a public space. Archie may have taken the small mountain

Top Left: *Dutch Olykoeks,* Albert Cuyp, oil, 1652, PD.

Top Right: *Traditional Inuit Bannock from Pangnirtung* photo Chan Mizuna.

Lower Left: *Buttermilk Donut Holes,* photo, fmloutdoors.com.

Lower Right: *Baking a Bannock in Scotland,* photo Sheri Nol.

works with him on his 1937 tour of the U.K. He visited his aunts Ada and Carrie Belaney that year—unbelievably as Grey Owl! Did he present his favourite mountain memories as gifts for the aunts who raised him? Maybe.

Hopefully, the scenarios with Tom and Archie in 1913 stimulate further research to prove or disprove their time together. In the meantime, it's great fun to speculate about two iconic Canadian figures—together!

Cabin, photo found in Grey Owl's old photos, AO-DBS, 1-273-1-0-4643.

There was a photo of an unidentified cabin found among Grey Owl's personal effects. He always had it with him.

Archie dressed for war dance, Archie at left, Harry Woodworth in middle, photo, AO-DBS, 1-273-1-0-46-41.

The Food Connection

The search for Tom Thomson's doughnut recipe raised many questions. Did he fry dollops of dough in a pan over the campfire, or wrap dough around a stick and place the stick over an open fire? Did he make doughnuts in a fry kettle on a stove in the ranger cabin at Lake Minisinakwa near Gogoma? Did he use his reflector oven? Where did he get the idea for doughnuts in the first place?

I tried to answer those questions by studying the history of doughnuts. Dutch *olykoeks*/oily cakes, made claims to be the ground zero of doughnuts. The Dutch had long deep fried oily cakes filled with apples, prunes and raisins; they had also tied their dough in knots, hence the term dough knots—later donuts.

The recipe for sweet dough balls fried in pork fat made a sea voyage to the new world very early on in the history of North America. These deep fried dough balls had a design flaw. Their centres frequently came out of the fry kettle insufficiently cooked. An unnamed doughnut engineer improved the design by increasing the surface area of the dough. This inventor simply cut a hole out of the centre of the dough to expose more surfaces to the hot oil. The inventive use for the middle bits was left for future generations to discover.

I loved this doughnut history but decided Tom had better antecedents than Dutch oily cakes. His Scottish ancestors had baked and fried dough for centuries—as bannock and oatcakes. Tom also knew Indian fry bread made by First Nations. Fried dough had a long history that transcended cultural divides.

From Tom's provision lists, we know he had the ingredients to make doughnuts: flour, baking powder, sugar, rendered bacon grease. One of his provision lists even had prunes for doughnut filling, if he so desired. The question remained: Which doughnut methodology did Tom Thomson use?

Ultimately, even after discussing this issue with several camp cooks, I could not answer the question. Instead, I turned to my own mouth-watering experiences with fried dough to imagine a doughnut scenario. The German New Year's Eve "Berliners" of my childhood were always filled with warm jam and they were rolled in sugar. For Archie Belaney to remember Tom's doughnuts two decades after eating them, I decided they too had to be sweet concoctions like my own Berliners, the memory of which made me drool 50 years later.

A picture started to form. I saw Tom with a berry pail scooping water from a northern river; he added sugar and baking soda to his flour before trickling in the water. Tom kneaded the dough with flour-covered hands and then dropped pucks of it into the long-handled frying pan of bacon grease that was heating up over the fire; maybe Archie was tending the fat. For a special treat, Tom placed a spoonful of his home-made strawberry preserve on some dough circles before folding and sealing them. When sufficiently browned, Tom took the fried dough balls and rolled them in a second pan in which the bottom was covered with sugar. He served the filled and unfilled donuts together making the preserve filling a surprise as special as getting the threepence coin in the traditional British plum pudding.

All this was imagination, of course. *The Toronto (Queen City of Canada) Cookbook* of 1915 has eight recipes for doughnuts. Here's one:

Raised Doughnuts

"Three pints flour, two-thirds cup butter, one and a half cup sugar, one cup yeast or half a yeast cake, salt and spice. Mix and let rise over night; on the morning, mix thoroughly and drop in small balls into the hot fat."

I love the rhyming recipe on page 45 of *The Toronto Cookbook:*

Doughnuts

"One cup of sugar, brown or white,
Now add an egg, and beat it light,
A little salt, with spice to taste,
Baking powder, too, must now be placed;
Three teaspoonfuls bought of Gillett,
I find as good as any yet,
One cup of milk, now stir together,
They will prove as light as any feather;
Just flour enough to roll them out,
But you must mind what you're about,
And keep your lard at proper heat—
You'll find these doughnuts hard to beat."

What is the heritage of your family's fried dough recipe?

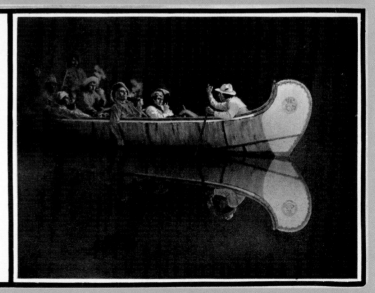

Above: Curtis Williamson. *Church Interior, 1896.* Oil on canvas, 53.7 x 46.3 cm (21 1/8 x 18 1/4 in.). Purchased with funds given by Mr. and Mrs. Wallace G. Chalmers and Ms. Joan Chalmers in commemoration of the 60th wedding anniversary of their parents, Dr. and Mrs. Floyd Chalmers, 1981. © Art Gallery of Ontario 2017.

Top Centre: *Franklin Carmichael's childhood home on Scott Street, Orillia,* photo excerpt from article by Sara Carson, "Committee seeks heritage designation for Group of Seven member's childhood home", *Orillia Packet & Times, June 18, 2013.*

Top and Middle Right: Photos of Franklin Carmichael from the Collection of Paul Gauthier.

Lower Right: "The Departure of the Fur Brigade", Arthur Heming, oil, from *The Drama of the Forests,* chapter eight, PD.

CHAPTER TWELVE

The Odd Couple, Franklin Carmichael and Tom

"*Tom Thomson and I have got married and we cook and share our meals together, giving half and half.*"

*Franklin Carmichael in a letter to his fiancée, Ada Lillian Went*cxxvii

Franklin Carmichael, photo, AO, F 1075-12-0-0-166.

From fall 1914 to fall 1915, Franklin Carmichael had up-close and personal views of Tom Thomson as cook. Except for Tom's travels, they worked, and sometimes lived together, in the Rosedale Valley for a year. In that time, Franklin shared meals with Tom and artists with sobriquets such as John Beatty, "the painting fireman"; Arthur Heming, "Chronicler of the North"; and Curtis Williamson, the "Canadian Rembrandt". These artists had earned their nicknames for exploits a decade or more before: John Beatty for 10 years as a City of Toronto fireman; Arthur Heming for over 6,000 miles (9,656 km) on northern tours by raft, dog team, snowshoes and canoe; and Curtis Williamson for bringing Dutch subject matter and painting techniques to Toronto in the 1890s. Their pasts comingled as tenants at The Studio Building. They were all part of the conversational brew that changed the flavour of Canadian art from European, to distinctly home-grown—possibly to the disgruntlement of a few of these same gentlemen artists who were more conservative than Tom and Franklin.

Franklin was 24-years-of age to Tom's 37 years when he and Tom first moved in together.[cxxviii] They'd met in 1911 when Franklin started as an office boy at Grip Limited for the underwhelming sum of $2.50 per week. In the subsequent years, like many of the Grip Limited crew, and his 12-year-older cousin, the painter Fred Haines[1] before him, Franklin took night courses with George Reid and William Cruikshank, the stalwarts of Toronto art education: Reid for his Life Class, and Cruikshank for Painting from the Antique.

Toronto Art Students' League, c. 1886
AO, F 1140-7-0-4.

The Grip Limited lads also took Franklin on sketching adventures to favourite haunts along the Humber River, in High Park, at York Mills and to other spots favoured over the years by successive sketching groups such as the Toronto Art Students' League (1886–1904) and the Mahlstick Club (1899–1904), clubs which blended into the Graphic Arts Club when the other two folded. Young Franklin might well have taken them sketching too. His aforementioned older cousin, Fred S. Haines,[cxxix] lived on Willow Lane in picturesque Meadowvale. The village was nestled among pine forests near the Credit River in Mississauga, Ontario. Meadowvale[cxxx] drew artists and photographers[cxxxi] to the shores of the river and with his cousin right there, Franklin had something special to offer his workmates. Thus, with helpful friends and wonderful art experiences, Franklin progressed from office boy, to Grip Limited apprentice and then to designer—a meteoric rise.

Franklin's rapid ascendancy sprang from a solid foundation that combined innate ability, family support and artistic mentoring. His mother, Susanna Eleanor Smith and her sister Martha Jane grew up in Meaford, Ontario. Franklin's aunt, Martha Jane gave birth to Frederick Stanley Haines in Meaford in 1879, and Susanna Eleanor had Franklin Carmichael in Orillia in 1890. The sisters encouraged the raw talent they saw in their sons and both developed into successful artists and art educators.

[1] Fred Haines owned Tom's work *Autumn Petawawa, Fall 1916.*

Hand carved eagle lectern,
Canon Greene, "A Walking Tour of St. James'
Anglican Church, Orillia".

Susannah enlisted Rev. Canon Richard W.E. Greene,[cxxxii] of St. James Anglican Church in Orillia, to provide art instruction for her precocious son. The multitalented rector had sketchbooks full of drawings from ecclesiastical postings in Ontario and the United States. Greene was a skilled watercolourist, and his hand-carved, eagle-themed lectern graced the church in which the Carmichaels worshipped. Canon Greene supervised Franklin's artistic interests and helped to develop his skills.

Franklin's father, David Graham Carmichael was a blacksmith by trade. He ran a carriage making shop in Orillia when Franklin was young. He took his son to his shop to watch and learn the fine craft of carriage making, a process that ended when scrollwork was added as decoration to the conveyances. The elder Carmichael rotated Franklin through all aspects of the trade, but Franklin took most to the design aspects, adding his steady hand to the fine decorative striping.

Cartier blacksmith shop in Burlington, Vermont, 1886, johnfishersr.net. The images gives an idea of a period blacksmith/carriage works such as David Graham Carmichael would have had.

Young Carmichael was not only artistically talented. He was otherwise precocious. He played the violin, cello, bassoon, piano and flute and immersed himself in advanced reading. One book in his large library,[cxxxiii] *Ralph Waldo Emerson: Essays and Other Writings*

(London, Cassel, 1907), was inscribed, Franklin Carmichael 1908. Franklin underscored much in this book but the chapter titled "The Over-Soul" was marked up the most. One item noted was, "God reappears with all his parts in every moss and cobweb." Had Franklin read this aloud to Tom when they were at rest in Studio One in the deep winter of 1914, Tom could have replied in the same vein with his Uncle Brodie's words: "Gather ye plant specimens whence ye may—from pine top or blade of grass, from *Ranunculus* to fungus—and ask the question fearlessly: 'Whose image and superscription is this?'"[cxxxiv] Both Tom and Franklin had influences that prompted them to seek deity in nature.

Another influence entered Franklin Carmichael's life in 1908 in the shape of Midland painter and etcher, William J. Wood. Before meeting Franklin, Wood had worked on the Great Lakes in international shipping and in the Midland Shipyards at a time when many ships for Great Lakes transport were constructed in Ontario. In 1908, Wood worked for the Herald Printing Company, stationers—and printers of the *Temiskaming Herald.* Wood produced illustrations for them and worked weekends on his own art. He had a small press in his modest home where he turned out etchings.

Eighteen-year-old Franklin made William Wood's acquaintance at the fall fair in Orillia in 1908 where both had works on exhibit. Not long after, Wood moved from Midland to Orillia to work in the Carmichael carriage shop.[cxxxv] The philosophical Wood was a sympathetic match for Franklin. Both at the carriage shop and outside work, the two had common interests. Wood encouraged Franklin's first foray into etching. Art historian John Hartman writes, "Soon after moving to Orillia, using his own equipment, he [Wood] helped Carmichael etch a plate. Wood commented, "The results are delightful."[cxxxvi] In a December 27, 1911 letter to Arthur Lismer, Wood thanks Lismer for the Christmas gift of the magazine *Saturday Night* and says that, "Franklin and I have had the pleasure of going over it together."[cxxxvii] Both Franklin and Wood dreamed of heading to Toronto to pursue art. Franklin left Orillia in 1911, as did Wood, but while Franklin stayed in Toronto, Wood returned to Midland in 1913. Ironically, they ended up in the same Toronto circles that led to the Group of Seven.

Franklin's enriched arts background at his father's shop, with Canon Greene and with William Wood, equipped him with a tremendous skill set and nudged him towards transcendental ideas. His gifts ensured rapid integration into the Grip Limited crowd. Based on his talents and disposition, it was easy to see why Franklin, Tom and J.E.H. became friends. The fact that Lawren Harris gave Franklin two books on theosophy in 1912–1913, shows the quiet, contemplative Franklin had another conversational partner to chat with about things spiritual and philosophical.

In 1913, Franklin decided to further his art education in Belgium. He and his cousin Fred Haines sailed to Antwerp to attend the *Academie Royal des Beaux Arts,* where Franklin's co-workers F. H. Varley and Arthur Lismer had studied. Haines earned a gold medal in figure studies in their first term there. Then came the start of WWI and the end of the cousins' study tour; they returned to Canada. As many of Franklin's Grip Limited colleagues had migrated to Rous and Mann Engravers during his overseas stay, Franklin went there as well.

John McLeish, in a biography of Arthur Lismer titled *September Gale,* relates a story that shows just how well Franklin was respected within the circle of artists and designers in Toronto. On the day Marjorie Lismer was born, May 16, 1913, Arthur and Esther Lismer had cash flow problems. They needed money to pay the hospital bill for their daughter's birth. "In the emergency, he telephoned Carmichael, who came up to the hospital with Tom Thomson, the two of them hurrying up from the centre of the city, having routed out enough money to tide over the crisis."[cxxxviii] The vignette shows Franklin and Tom acting in tandem; it also shows Franklin as a trusted friend.

Young Woman with White Cap, 1890, Albert Curtis Williamson, Collection of the WAG; Gift of Mrs. P.A. Chester through the Women's Committee.

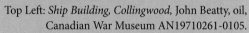

Top Left: *Ship Building, Collingwood,* John Beatty, oil,
Canadian War Museum AN19710261-0105.

Centre Right: "Helen Blavatsky", illustration, *The Lamp,* May 15, 1895,
the torontoist.com. Blavatsky was considered an important figure
among Toronto's theosophists.

Far Right: *"In Port"* W.J. Wood, drawing, Huronia Museum.

Lower Right: *Shipyards and Dry Dock, Midland, Ontario,* PD.
W.J. Wood worked at the shipyards for a while; artist John Beatty painted there.

In 1913, Lawren Harris raised a new prospect. Harris and Dr. James MacCallum were funding the construction of The Studio Building on Severn Street in the Rosedale Valley. They hoped to establish an artists' community to further the nascent Canadian vision in art they'd seen in the works of J.E.H. MacDonald, Tom Thomson and A.Y. Jackson. The Studio Building promised to be an exciting venue—a nexus between the old and the new in Canadian art.

Tom Thomson moved into the building even before it was completely finished in January 1914. He shared workspace with A.Y. Jackson. However just a month later, A.Y. went off to paint in Algonquin Park and then when WWI started, he wrote to say he wanted to join up. Although Jackson offered to continue to pay his share, Tom looked for other possibilities, including Arthur Lismer. He finally enlisted Franklin to move in to share the $22 a month rent of Studio One. Franklin liked Tom and welcomed the opportunity to share work space in the exciting new community.

However, even at the reduced rate of $11 per month, Studio One was not suited to Tom's pocket book. He had loved the rustic park ranger shelter cabins he'd visited on his 1912 and 1913 trips to Muskoka, the

Bark Lake Ranger Cabin, photo, AO-DBS, 1-273-1-0-50-22.

Ranger Cabin, Green Lake, photo, AO-DBS, 1-273-1-0-50-16.

Historic spot in the annals of Canadian art is Tom Thomson's shack, behind the Studio Building in Toronto. It is once more serving as a creative centre. Frances Gage, young Candian sculptress, is using it as a studio. Here, she surveys the picturesque setting. —*See story on Page 65.*

—Richard Cole, Globe and Mail.

"Historic Spot", photo, Richard Cole, *Globe and Mail,* clipping undated, courtesy of Rebecca Middleton.

Mississagi and Mattagami areas and sought more basic accommodation. To keep him connected to the new artists' colony in the Rosedale Valley, Dr. MacCallum spent $176 to refurbish a dilapidated workman's shed on the east side of the building. Tom moved into this suitably rustic abode at the rental rate of $1 a month—much easier on the pocketbook and a damn sight more primitive.

In deep winter 1915, Tom moved to The Shack. Lawren Harris in *The Story of the Group of Seven,* wrote, "We fixed it up, put down a new floor, made the roof watertight, built in a studio window, put in a stove, and electric light. Tom made himself a bunk, shelves, a table, and a easel, and lived in that place as he would in a cabin in the north."[cxxxix] Tom, Franklin and other visitors cooked meals on a wood-burning stove, the pipe of which was rigged overhead to route outside. Tom's shelves held the preserves he made from fruit brought or shipped from the north; his fishing lures, rods and paraphernalia decorated the walls. Paintings hung and leaned everywhere. Tom's favourite Hudson's Bay tobacco smoke clouded the air.

Unbeknownst to Tom, Franklin was looking to change his living situation. He was deeply in love with Ada Lillian Went. Franklin's fiancée had grown up on Penetang

Street in Orillia with her father James, stepmother Elizabeth Beard, and three brothers from Edward's first wife, Lucy Bromwich. Lucy had died in 1891, most likely in childbirth with Ada. When Elizabeth Beard gave birth to baby Ruby in 1896, and baby Hazel in 1899, duties for Ada increased. By the 1911 census of Ontario, Ada no longer lived with her father and stepmother.

Boxing Match in Riverdale Ravine, photo, CTA Fonds 1244, 9718.

The frugal Franklin saved up as rapidly as he could so that he could marry Ada. In his frequent letters from The Studio Building he diverted her with talk of the cast of characters who made up life at The Shack and in the studios. He told her that Dr. MacCallum, the patron saint of the building, had dropped by; they'd had breakfast with Arthur Heming; "Bill" Beatty came and fried potatoes; he was preparing Irish stew in a casserole pot. He'd burnt his fingers. He told her of playing chess and having tea with Arthur up in his studio and of going to a boxing match near Broadview Avenue and King Street with Dr. MacCallum and Arthur. He said that for everyone's entertainment Tom had made his mulligan stews that sputtered while Tom stirred and cursed. They had toasted homemade bread over open embers. Clearly it was a great bachelor year.

By May 1915, Franklin had saved enough to get married and set up a new household. He wrote Tom about his marriage plans. Tom replied from up north that Franklin should take anything he wanted from The Shack as wall decoration for the new home the couple would have. Franklin wrote Ada that he loved Tom's works enough to clear the place out, but he took just two pieces: *Hoar Frost* from spring 1914 and *Forest Interior, 1912.* Ada and Franklin's marriage was solemnized September 15, 1915.

Top Left: *Carmichael Famly*, Clarence (brother), Franklin holding his daughter Mary, unknown man and David (father). Paul Gauthier Collection.

Top Right: *Radial car headed south from Lansing*, 1918, TPL.

Lower Left: *Building Franklin Carmichael's cabin in Cranberry Bay*, 1934, Willisville Photo Gallery.

Lower Right: *Franklin Carmichael, La Cloche #2*, oil on wood panel, 24.5x29.8cm, Collection of the Tom Thomson Art Gallery, Owen Sound, purchased with assistance from the Province of Ontario Council for the Arts, 1967.

Tom didn't like his 'divorce' from Franklin. Franklin wrote Ada on May 25, 1915, "Poor old boy, the whole tone of his letter seemed to be so blue. I wanted to rush up to the park just to have a chat with him and cheer him up a bit."[cxl]

In very late fall, Tom returned to single life. Franklin commuted to Rous and Mann from Thornhill where he'd rented a house in the same area as J.E.H. MacDonald. He was happy in his new domestic sphere— that is, until he heard that his good friend Tom had died. In 1920 Franklin had saved sufficiently to purchase a bungalow in the village of Lansing. Ada and Franklin's daughter Mary was born August 3, 1921. Franklin did not rejoin his old pals on painting trips right away as he loved being with his new family.

In the 1930s Franklin and Ada rented and then bought a cottage in the La Cloche Hills, an area in Northeastern Ontario that sprawled near Killarney and Sudbury. Franklin had loved the white quartzite rock landscape since he'd first visited the region in the teen years of the century. But for the loss of his dear friend Tom, Franklin Carmichael's dreams had come true.

The Food Connection

Franklin Carmichael's mother, Susannah Smith Carmichael, had an Irish heritage but based on his March 23, 1915, letter to his fiancée, Ada Went, it's unlikely Franklin learned to cook Irish stew from her. He wrote, "I have just finished preparing an Irish stew, to be cooked not like an ordinary stew, but in a casserole pot, so we are anxiously waiting to see what the results of this experiment will be."

The experimental nature of Franklin's stew rules out the need to imagine him following in the footsteps of precursor Celts brewing mutton in cauldrons over peat fires. Franklin probably prepared his stew from a basic recipe of the period. Just as Tom would have used rendered bacon or pork fat for his camp cooking, Franklin would have rendered the lamb fat to brown the lamb meat for the stew. Other traditional ingredients were onions, potatoes and thyme. Chopped parsley and melted butter were traditional finishing touches. After those basics, the ingredients become controversial. Purists eschew carrots, parsnips and turnip, and prefer lamb stock to beef or chicken stock.

Franklin's casserole approach reflects the many recipes that layer lamb and root vegetables—mostly with the potatoes ending up on top to steam them. Recipes call for each layer to be handily sprinkled with thyme or just salt and pepper. Just as Tom's mulligan stew was as creative as the ingredients, Franklin's Irish stew has lots of scope for invention. One of many available period recipe follows.

Mrs. Beeton's Irish Stew

"Ingredients: 3 lbs of neck of mutton, 4 lbs of potatoes, 1 large onion, 12 button onions,

1 ½ pints of stock or water, salt and pepper, a little finely chopped parsley.

Method: Cut the meat into pieces convenient for serving, and trim off some of the fat. Wash, peel, and slice the potatoes and the large onion, peel the button onions and blanch them. Put a layer of potatoes at the bottom of a stew pan, cover these with a layer of meat, add a slice or two of onion, and season well with salt and pepper. Repeat until all the materials are used; the top layer must consist of potato, and the button onions should be interspersed. Add the stock or water and when it comes to the boil, skim well, but unless the meat be very fat, very little subsequent skimming is needed as

the potatoes absorb the greater part melted out of the meat. The stew pan must be kept covered, and the contents cooked gently for about 1 ½ hours, or until the potatoes are thoroughly cooked and the stew loses its watery appearance. If liked, a teaspoonful of mushroom or walnut ketchup may be added before serving. Pile in the centre of a hot dish, sprinkle on a little chopped parsley, and serve."

Bloor Viaduct under construction, Don Section, Pier E, September 21, 1915. TPL Bloor Viaduct Album BV 611.

Now for an imaginary glimpse of Franklin at work in The Shack in January 1915. Tom has just left to snow-shoe through the Rosedale Ravine to the Don River Valley to check out the site where construction of a new bridge is underway. Franklin stands at the stove to stir the simmering lamb stock he started the day before with a kilo of lamb bones. He takes the mutton cubes he's already chopped and rinsed. They're in a colander in a porcelain ewer—to get rid of the last blood residue. That's right. Franklin has mutton, not lamb. Mutton is cheaper because it comes from older sheep. He and Tom made jokes yesterday about just how old and worn out a sheep has to be to proceed from lamb to mutton.

Well, that's enough. You get the picture.

William Davis store, 1910, photo, CTA Fonds 1244, it0339a.

Tom Thomson, *Hoar Frost 1914*, oil on canvas adhered to paperboard, 22.4x26.8cm, Gift of Mr. C.A.G. Matthews, McMichael Canadian Art Collection, 1968.25.21. Franklin and Ada received this from Tom Thomson for their wedding.

CHAPTER THIRTEEN

John William Beatty, a Boisterous Friend

"At the age of 13 he was expelled for putting a dead chicken on his teacher's desk and he told his parents he had no intention of returning." Dorothy Hoover, *J.W. Beatty*, 1948

John William Beatty, photo, AO F 1075-12-0-0-4.

Among Tom Thomson's friends and acquaintances, the fiery John Beatty[1] was by far the most outgoing. Right from his expulsion from Phoebe Street Public School,[cxli] the boisterous lad, the fifth of sign painter Samuel Beatty's[cxlii] nine children, raced through life with a rapacious appetite for new experiences.

By the time Tom met him in 1910, John Beatty had already earned his papers as a journeyman painter; been a bugle boy with No. 1 Company of the 10th Grenadiers when they repressed the 1885 Northwest Rebellion of Louis Riel; headed a paint shop in Minneapolis; he'd driven horses for 10 years in the hook and ladder days of Toronto's first fire service. He'd also married Caroline Cornock of Caledon,[cxliii] a "good looking waitress at the Schulyer Hotel across the street from the Lombard Street Fire Hall,"[cxliv] and studied at the *Académie Julien* in Paris. Upon his return from France, he took over the muralist Frederick Challener's[cxlv] studio at 43 Adelaide Street in Toronto in an area then referred to as the Montparnasse of Toronto. In this new milieu Beatty worked among struggling artists and gave some lessons.

Beatty's artistic endeavours began during his 10 year (1889–1900) career as Toronto's "painting fireman". During slow times in fire fighting, Beatty painted portraits in a studio he'd carved out of the upstairs rooms of the Lombard Street Fire Hall. He took time to amuse the public with stunts sliding down the fireman's pole, sometimes head first and sometimes with

---

[1]*John Beatty was also known as William Beatty, J.W. Beatty and Bill Beatty.*

Left: *Morning, Algonquin Park, 1914,* John Beatty, Collection of Shane and Troy Beggs. Courtesy of the Oeno Gallery, thanks to Carlyn Moulton.

Top Right: *March Evening Northland,* J.E.H. MacDonald, oil, 1914, PD.

Lower Right: *Frozen Lake, Early Spring, Algonquin Park, 1914,* A.Y. Jackson, oil, 1914, PD.

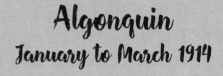

Algonquin
January to March 1914

a fellow fireman on his back, a trick he repeated for the Duke of Connaught[cxlvi] in 1890 when the Duke visited the Free Masons' Ionic Lodge in Toronto.

John W. Beatty, J.E. Sampson, drawing, Arts and Letters Club Archive courtesy of Scott James.

James Elliott in a *Windsor S*tar article called Beatty a boisterous Orangeman, a wild carouser and an *enfant terrible*[cxlvii]. The art critic Augustus Bridle, (member #1 of the Arts and Letters Club) a contemporary of Beatty said of him that, "He was a glorious, truculent bigot, ready for action with either fists or vocabulary."[cxlviii] Bridle waxed poetic on other occasions calling Beatty a cyclone of speed and a cataract of glowing energy. Beatty's friends best remembered him as the centre of verbal combat.[cxlix]

Tom Thomson did not cross paths with the colourful Beatty at this point. John and Caroline Beatty were set to embark on a second study trip to Europe just as Tom was getting established in Toronto. The Beattys came back to Toronto in January 1909. From that point on, Tom had many possibilities to meet John—not the least of which would have been through Tom's new boss, Albert Robson, the Art Director at Grip Limited.

John Beatty and Albert Robson became brothers-in-law on December 23, 1907 when Robson married Mildred Jeanette Cornock, a younger sister to Beatty's wife Caroline. Had Albert Robson shown his brother-in-law around the Grip Limited offices, upon the latter's return to Toronto, he would have met the recently employed Tom Thomson. However, that need not be the way they met. Beatty was good friends with J.E.H. MacDonald back to their Mahlstick Club sketching times at the beginning of the century[cl]. Tom was friends with J.E.H. in 1907 even before he became his supervisor in the Grip Limited Art Department. There can be little doubt that with J.E.H. as a common friend Beatty and Thomson would soon be acquainted. Only Beatty's many travels in 1909 stood in the way of Tom and John meeting that year. Beatty raced out into the wilds after his lengthy stay abroad.

Top Left: *En route Mattagami* photo, AO, 57662.

Top Right: *The Duke of Connaught visits the Toronto Street Temple, Ionic Lodge, May 30, 1890,* photo, PD.

Lower Left: *Mahlstick Club, 1899–1902,* photo, Colgate Papers, AO.

In spring 1909, Beatty was on the move with his Arts and Letters friend, Lawren Harris. The pair travelled to Haliburton to sketch; in the fall they explored Lake Memphremagog on the Quebec–Vermont border—both times from a canoe. Beatty made time in August to be with his friend Frederick Challener at his barn in Conestoga, north of Kitchener, where Challener painted his large murals. Even later that fall, Beatty travelled to the Mattagami area[cli] with Tom (Thomas Wesley) McLean, an early member of the Arts and Letters Club and another employee of Grip Limited. The October 30, 1909, *Globe* reported in a column titled, "Views of the World: what artists are doing" that, "An almost virgin field for artists was visited by Mr. J.W. Beatty and Mr. T. W. McLean who spent some weeks in the vicinity of Fort Mattagami, in Northern Ontario."[clii]

Canoe on the Missisagi, 1910, A-DBS, 1-273-1-0-50-9.

THE LATE NEIL McKECHNIE

"Neil McKechnie", Memorial Booklet, TRL.

Perhaps, McLean wanted to revisit the site where his pal and Grip Limited workmate Neil McKechnie drowned while on a canoe trip with him in 1904[cliii] but it's more likely that he and Beatty were fired with determination to find inspiration for art in Canada. According to Beatty's biographer, Dorothy Hoover, Beatty said after his visits north that year, "I discovered enough material on the fringes of the Ontario Northland to make me forget the Old World for the rest of my days."[cliv]

Hoover places Tom Thomson and John Beatty together just shortly after Beatty exhibited *Evening*

151

Cloud of the Northland in 1910. She describes them first of all as practical jokers. With John's background —sliding down the fire hall pole head first—it's easy to see how he sparked Tom's prankish side. Hoover also notes they were great canoeists and woodsmen and that their friendship led to many sketching trips together.[clv] Hoover indicates it was during a sketching trip with Thomson that Beatty collected the material for *First Snow in the Woods.*[clvi] A.Y. Jackson corroborated that these sketching trips took place in a eulogy for Beatty in 1941. Jackson said that he had heard the pair talk of their times together.[clvii]

It's certain that 'northern fever' had fully gripped Tom Thomson by 1912. He went on two trips that summer, one to Algonquin and the other along the Mississagi River. Thereafter, Tom stayed north as much as the weather and finances allowed.

In 1913 to 1914 another adventure unfolded. Tom, A.Y. Jackson, John Beatty and J.E.H. MacDonald moved into The Studio Building even before it was officially opened in January 1914. Beatty immediately undertook the supervision of the carpenters, painters and steam fitters.[clviii] Tom watched that drama unfold.

Within a month of moving into the new quarters, and maybe because of the hubbub, A.Y. Jackson was off to Algonquin Park. Jackson scouted on snowshoes for scenery to paint. He was joined for 10 days, during February/March, by J.E.H. MacDonald and John Beatty who were likewise inspired by the winter scenes. Hoover reports that Beatty, "took a keen delight in sketching at 20 below zero without even wearing gloves. More than once the ends of his fingers were frost bitten."[clix] The works from that winter trip convey the deeply chilled experiences these men had. A.Y. Jackson, *Frozen Lake, Early Spring, Algonquin Park* shows an ice covered lake; J.E.H. MacDonald *March Evening Northland 1914* is dominated by snow-laden, storm clouds and Beatty's *Morning, Algonquin Park, 1914*[clx] features snow and bare trees. Within a month, Tom followed his friends into Algonquin Park. We see that it was still cold in April. There is much snow in his painting of Lowery Dickson's Shack at the mouth of Potter and Joe Creeks near Canoe Lake.

Tom stayed on in Algonquin Park for the spring of 1914 and then headed to the Parry Sound and the French River area to camp with Dr. MacCallum and later to stay at the latter's cottage on Georgian Bay. He did not join A.Y. Jackson, Beatty and C.W. Jefferys on their great western adventure. They had a commission from the Canadian Northern Railroad to capture scenes of the railway's construction through the Rockies—for advertising purposes. Beatty, with his usual enthusiasm, painted along the rail line, at stations and from the trains—all the while making friends. Tom was in transit from Georgian Bay to South River while Beatty chatted up railway workers. Jackson told everyone afterwards that the loquacious Beatty made a huge number of friends in every construction camp they visited.[clxi]

Tom caught up with his friends in September and October. Beatty, Jackson, Lismer and Varley all came to Algonquin Park. There were tales and discussions, some in Mowat Lodge and others over campfires and in canoes. Tom learned that Jackson was not fond of the works he'd painted for the railroad commission but that Beatty was rapturous. Tom caught Beatty's enthusiasm. From that point on he talked frequently about going west to paint the Rockies.

Tom and Beatty became co-chefs in November 1915 when Tom changed his living quarters to The Shack. They shared meals, talked of art and had fun. Franklin Carmichael tells of Beatty making his specialty, oyster stew. Beatty probably had a family recipe, as oysters were popular among the frugal classes when John was a boy and North American oyster beds thrived. In the

late 1890s a survey of barges in New York Harbour found over six million oysters. By the time John cooked his oyster stew for Tom and others on the wood-burning stove in The Shack, oysters were in decline from over-harvesting, disease, and the destruction of their oyster beds. The hungry Shack crew would have enjoyed what had, by 1915, become a delicacy.

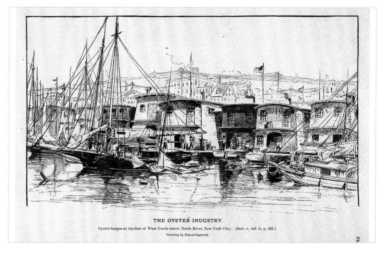

THE OYSTER INDUSTRY.
Oyster-barges at the foot of West Tenth street, North River, New York City. (Sect. v, vol. ii, p. 355.)
Drawing by Ernest Ingersoll

Oyster Industry Postcard, PD.

For seven years Tom and John were connected through common enthusiasms, common friends, The Studio Building and The Shack. Hoover relates that, "When Thomson was hard up, Beatty helped in more than one occasion to raise money by selling his sketches for him, or by giving him a meal." William

Little quotes Dorothy Stone in *The Tom Thomson Mystery,* as saying*,* "Another example of Tom's pride was that he would never admit if he were broke or hungry and times he would land in on Beatty at The Studio Building straight off the evening train from the North. Beatty would ask if he had had any supper—"of course he had!" So Beatty would remark that he had been working past his meal time and would Thomson keep him company while he went out for a bite and they would go down to Bloor and Yonge and have a couple of big steaks and Thomson's pride was saved."[clxii] The Art Gallery of Ontario website entry for Thomson's *Autumn Scene,* 1916, states that. "It is possible that Thomson gave this painting to Beatty because they were such good friends."

In 1917, John Beatty was devastated when Tom died. He dedicated tremendous energy to the construction of the Tom Thomson Cairn on Canoe Lake. J.E.H. MacDonald wrote to Tom's father that, "Mr. Beatty planned the cairn and directed and did most of the work with its erection. Most of the stone had to be carried up a steep cliff about 60 feet (18m) high."[clxiii] Beatty hauled up all the sand too. Augustus Bridle noted in *The Story of the Club* that, "Thomson's death 'left an emotional scar on Bill's life'."[clxiv] (Close friends called John William Beatty, Bill.)

Students with J.W. Beatty, left, at Port Hope Summer School, 1923, OCAD Visual Resources and Special Collections, PH119/57__004_367_019.

The amicable John Beatty, nevertheless, carried on. He taught at the Ontario College of Art and was an official WWI War Artist on the front Lines in France; he exhibited in the British Empire Exhibition in London, the *Jeu de Paume* in Paris and in many prominent places. He started and taught an Ontario College of Art Summer school that influenced generations of teachers.

When John Beatty passed away in 1941, his erstwhile critic Augustus Bridle wrote that his later paintings, "… were not the work of an oldish man … but the amazing panorama of one man's unkillable love of the Canadian scene."[clxv] At his funeral his militia buddies from 1885 gave him a final salute. Had he lived, Tom would have saluted John Beatty for all the good times they had together.

Ablain-St. Nazaire, John William Beatty, oil, Canadian War Museum.

The Food Connection

"Only December guaranteed enough sustained cold weather for shipping. Then, from Baltimore, to Charleston, to New Orleans, oysters were shoveled onto the flat backs of horse-drawn wagons and packed down in wet straw and seaweed for an inland journey sometimes lasting two weeks or more. Far from the coast, oysters became a symbol of the arrival of the winter holiday season, appearing in the markets by Christmas Eve and on the tables that night as oyster stew." Bill Neal, *Bill Neal's Southern Cooking,* 1989.

Still Life with Oysters, Alexander Adriaenssen, 1630s. PD.

In ancient Rome and Greece, oysters made their appearance as aphrodisiacs. The First Nations of North American harvested oysters to such a degree that oyster shell mounds greeted the first settlers as heaps on the shores of the continent. In the mid-19th century, Irish immigrants

125. MOONLIGHT
Tom Thomson

7. THE NORTH LAND.
"J. W. Beatty."

Top: *Low Water, Pig River*, photo, AO 57591.

Left: *Ontario Society of Artists Programmes featuring the works of Tom Thomson 1916 and J.W. Beatty 1912.*

promoted the tradition of Christmas Eve oyster stew, based on the Roman Catholic custom that no meat is served the day before a religious feast. In the cold season in Toronto whenever oysters arrived by rail, the oyster stew season began.

Peering into The Shack at McMichael Canadian Art Collection, photo Mary Cook.

As the son of Irish immigrants from the Ulster region, John Beatty grew up with oyster stew. It was a festive meal for him— one he would have gladly shared with his mates from The Studio Building. The ingredients were simple and the stew quickly made. While John made the stew, Tom could easily have made biscuits or bannock. It's fun picturing the men in The Shack as the smell of oyster milk wafts in the air.

The Home Cookbook: compiled by the ladies of Toronto and chief cities and towns in Canada provides several variants on oyster stew.

Mrs. Andrews Stewed Oysters

"In all cases, unless shell oysters, wash and drain; mix half a cup of butter and a tablespoon of corn starch, put with oysters in a porcelain kettle; stir until they boil; add two cups of cream or milk; salt to taste; do not use the liquor of the oysters in either stewing or escalloping."

Mrs. A.S. Ewing's Oyster Stew for Breakfast

"Strain the juice from the oysters placed in the colander into a stew pan; let it come to a boil; remove the scum and clear liquid will remain; turn cold water upon the oysters and rinse thoroughly; add them to the liquor with a cup of cream or milk, butter, salt and cayenne pepper. Have ready buttered, dice-shaped pieces of toast upon a meat dish; pour the oysters over, garnish with parsley, and serve hot."

The Every Day Cook Book and Encyclopedia of Practical Recipes by Miss E. Neil, published by Regan Printing House in Chicago in 1892, offers another variant.

157

Left: *Firemen,* John Beatty, photo of an oil, 1909, Art Gallery of Ontario, vertical file.

Right: *The Cook,* photo, AO 57570.

Oysters Stewed with Milk

"Take a pint of fine oysters, put them with their own liquor and a gill of milk into a stew pan, and if liked a blade of mace, set it over the fire, take off any scum which may rise; when they are plump and white, turn them into a deep plate; add a bit of butter, and pepper to taste. Serve crackers and dressed celery with them. Oysters may be stewed in their own liquor without milk."

A blade of mace and a gill of milk

Both Izaak Walton (*The Compleat Angler*) and Miss Neil above, used a 'blade of mace'. Nutmeg and mace blade come from the same evergreen tree which grows in the Spice Islands of Indonesia but also grows on the Island of Grenada in the Caribbean. Mace blade is the outer, bright orange/red, lace-like covering of the seed that becomes dark yellow/brown when dried. Mace blade has a sweeter, stronger taste than nutmeg. Mace is more expensive because a pile of fruit large enough to make 100 pounds (45 kg) of nutmeg produces one pound (.45 kg) of mace.

A gill is a unit of measurement for volume. One gill is equal to a quarter of a pint or approximately five ounces. In days of yore, the Royal Navy used to issue each man over 21-years-of-age, a daily gill of neat rum. Yo ho, mateys!

From Left: *Gill measure,* photo, *Grenada Nutmeg,* photo, *a blade of mace* photo by John Connell, 2009.

Tom Wattie with Sandbread, photo courtesy of Keith Thornborrow.

CHAPTER FOURTEEN

Tom Wattie, South River and the Postmistress

This chapter is dedicated to historian Keith Thornborrow who spent many hours in conversation with Wattie family members and period witnesses. He copied numerous photos and recorded the stories and anecdotes of several descendants of Tom Wattie. Keith generously shared his South River collection and his stories.

Tom Thomson loved much about South River: the goods at the South River Mercantile Co., the veneer panels from the National Wood Manufacturing Co. Ltd., and Algonquin Park Ranger Tom Wattie who introduced him to his family and the town's fairs, picnics and dances. Tom especially liked hitting the dance floor with South River's beautiful postmistress, Alice Smyth.[clxvi] That's not to say he didn't have his eye on other town beauties.

According to South River artist Brenda Scott, Tom frequently sat on the Hunter Street porch of Richard McGrath[clxvii] drinking tea with his lovely daughter Edna.[clxviii] He also talked art with Evelyn Ard, one of shopkeeper W.J. Ard's comely daughters. Evelyn had gone to Havergal Private School in Toronto and was in art classes at the Central Ontario School of Art and Design when Tom was a student there.[clxix] They had a great deal to talk about—stories of Cruikshank and classmates.

South River's allure drew Tom four times in as many years. Tom visited Wattie's ranger cabin, Idol Wild on Tea Lake, even more times than that for fishing, guiding and sketching expeditions.[clxx] Tom's friendship with Wattie started in August 1913, just after Tom had spent time as a fire ranger on the Mattagami Reserve south of Timmins in the company of Archie Belaney.[clxxi] Wattie took Tom to meet his family at their summer home on Round Lake (now Lake Kawawaymog). Tom was instantly captured by the charm of the Wattie clan; he was especially fond of eight-year-old Gordon and the rambunctious eleven-year-old Amelia, who the family called "Tootsie". With her Brownie box camera strung around her neck, Amelia poked around everywhere, offering commentary. Tom gave her tasks to keep her busy—cleaning brushes and such.

In town, Tom bought his first veneer boards, sized to his paint box. The thin three-ply boards were birch wood front and back and softer pine inside; they were expertly cut to size with a rotary saw. The Ard's General Store (also called the South River Lumber and Mercantile Company) stocked them, but they were from the National Wood Manufacturing Co. Ltd. that manufactured charcoal briquettes, wood alcohol and other distillates. Since hunter and fishermen came up to South River by the trainload, Ard's store, catered to all needs, from those of the locals to those of visiting outdoorsmen and artists. Vincent's Store was the alternative for some items and the South River Young Men's Annual Balls were held in the Vincent's Upstairs Hall.

In 1913 Tom didn't visit the Wattie's home on Ottawa Avenue in town or Tom Wattie's cabin on Round Lake or his "camp" on an island in the lake. He went from his hotel in South River back to where he'd camped with his friend Harry Jackson the previous summer, and then by portage to Canoe Lake where Shannon and Annie Fraser had officially opened Camp Mowat as Mowat Lodge. Tom had much to reflect upon as he camped, fished and painted around Canoe Lake that fall. The Ontario Government had purchased his painting, *A Northern Lake* from the Ontario Society of Arts exhibition that March. Its $250 purchase price opened a surprising door. Might he consider art as a livelihood?

The winter, spring and summer of 1914 led to many changes that reflected Tom's consideration of life as a professional artist. He moved to The Studio Building to share Studio One with A.Y. Jackson; he took up

Dr. MacCallum's offer of sponsorship. He also took a two month leave from Rous and Mann.

In the spring 1914, Tom visited Canoe Lake with Arthur Lismer—an Algonquin Park novice. He camped with him on Molly's Island in Smoke Lake and then headed through Ragged Lake to Crown and Wolf Lakes. Since the latter two lakes were slightly outside the park, Tom could hunt as well as fish for their meals. After Lismer's visit, Tom painted in the Georgian Bay area in the environs of the MacCallum cottage on Go Home Bay. He found life there too social—too much like Rosedale,[clxxii] he commented. He meant the posh neighbourhood and not the forested ravine in mid-Toronto. By August, he needed time out. He set his sights on a solo canoe journey that would take him from Georgian Bay, up the French River, across Lake Nipissing and along the South River to Algonquin Park; if he survived, he'd stop to visit Tom Wattie.

Arriving safely in South River, Tom started a tab at Ard's store. After a visit with his favourite small Watties—Tootsie and Gord—the two Toms withdrew to the quiet of Wattie's camp on the island in Round Lake. They fished, hunted and talked over the campfire—the way men do. With the heady changes Tom contemplated, his finances were foremost on his mind. He worried about having adequate funds for the future.

Wattie would have had suggestions. For years he'd made extra money with his sideline—guiding fishing and hunting expeditions from Idol Wild on Tea Lake. The hunting parties had to be outside the park, but eager fishermen and hunters paid well for guided adventures. Wattie had tourist 'patter', favourite fishing spots and a specialty, sand bread. Wattie's visitors loved to see him make his puffy, pan bread. Tom had his own unique talents. He was an exceptionally skilled fisherman, made a mean partridge stew, and could hunt with the best of them.

Tom grew up with guns and hunted as a youth. His sister Louisa said he was expert with a shotgun and rifle, and his childhood pal Allan Ross said he always had a gun across his lap when they were out fishing. Tom could skin and clean a squirrel, or pluck and clean a duck as fast as he filleted a salmon trout. Tom did not shoot deer but he did shoot small game and fowl—especially partridge. The previous summer, he and William Smithson Broadhead had hunted while they made their way down the Mississagi River. Fishing was Tom's true passion, but he was ready to hunt if the occasion arose.

Indeed, the summer of 1912, after Harry Jackson left, Tom guided Leonard E. Mack[clxxiii] and Harry Bracken on a fishing expedition from Canoe Lake through other lakes and portages to Crown Lake just outside the park, for hunting. Tom had the requisite skills to make guiding a lucrative sideline.

The Watties on Tea Lake, photo courtesy of Keith Thornborrow.

Before Tom departed for Canoe Lake in August of 1914, he visited the Ard store to pick up veneer panels. Tom had two dozen veneer boards custom cut by the National Wood Manufacturing Co. to 12"x9" (30x23 cm) for Lismer's paint box.[clxxiv] While in town, Tom probably took time for courtesy calls to South

River friends, Edna McGrath, Alice Smyth and Evelyn Ard. Then with a goodbye to the rest of the Watties at Ottawa Avenue, Tom headed to his fall appointments.

A.Y. Jackson and John Beatty were back from their Canadian Northern Railroad painting adventure out west in the Rockies. They were headed to see Tom in Algonquin. Arthur Lismer was returning to the Park with Esther and baby Marjorie, and Fred Varley was coming up with his wife Maud. It was going to be a painting party par excellence. The men didn't know it at the time, but it was also the end of an era. WWI would tear them apart.

Whereas Tom had worried if he'd have to walk rather than ride home from Algonquin in the fall of 1914,[clxxv] by 1915 he was flush. He'd downsized to The Shack at the rental rate of $1 a month; he'd earned $500 from the sale of *Northern River* to the National Gallery, and he had prospects for guiding.

Tom arrived at Tea Lake in mid-March 1915 to check out his schedule with Tom Wattie. He and guide George Rowe would take out American tourists in April; he and park ranger Bud Callighen had tourists lined up for mid-July and late fall, Wattie and he would take out a local South River doctor, Robert A. McComb, for hunting and fishing. In between jobs, Tom could canoe, fish and paint.

Art historians agree that Tom bought his new 16-foot (4.88 metre), Chestnut cruiser canoe, called the Guide's Special, or "the Boone", that summer. The Chestnut Co. of New Brunswick supplied retailers with catalogues from which they could order canoes. Since the South River Lumber & Mercantile Co., or Ard's, was a large outfitter, it's possible that Tom bought the canoe there on one of his many trips through the area that season. The custom, dove grey paint job he gave the canoe came from a $2 tube of cobalt blue artist's paint. Tom mixed the cobalt blue with canoe enamel.[clxxvi] Tom loved that canoe. Dr. R. P. Little in his "Recollections of Tom Thomson and Canoe Lake" said, "What a horse is to a cowboy, a 16-foot canvas covered canoe[1] is to Tom."[clxxvii]

For certain, Tom was in South River for Labour Day as he wrote Dr. MacCallum from the New Queen's Hotel on September 8, 1915.[clxxviii] He told the doctor he'd done about 100 sketches up to then, which he felt was a meagre output due to his busy summer. However, as he and Wattie weren't taking Dr. McComb hunting until November, he had more time for sketching and socializing.

In all his visits to the area, Tom had not yet been in town for the South River Agricultural Fair, a grand event that took place each year in the second week of September. There was a parade and the judging of everything from stock, poultry, cabbage heads, jars of pickles and jams, to 50 lb. (23 kg) firkins of butter. The fair ended with a box social and a dance that featured a local band. Tom had postmistress Alice Smyth, his favourite partner, to twirl around the dance floor, but Edna McGrath would have pined for his attention as well. Edna was 30-years-old, and according to Brenda Scott, very serious about Tom's porch and parlour visits. She took them for courting.[clxxix] Alice, on the other hand, at 19-years-of-age enjoyed the fun and the attention. With many men off to war in September 1915, there were lots of other women watching from the wings. The Ard sisters alone numbered three: Eleanor, Evelyn and Alma, not to mention Tootsie Wattie, who in 1915 was 13 and had a teenage crush on Tom.

Tom left South River for a while after the fair, venturing towards Mattawa. He had almost a month to paint fall scenes. When it was finally time to collect Dr. McComb,

[1] *photo of canoe on page 164*

Left: *South River Mercantile Company.*
Photo, courtesy of Keith Thornborrow.

Right: *Shannon Fraser is the man standing in black,
with Tom's famous dove-grey canoe in front of him*
Photo Sylvia (Hayhurst) Telford.

BOUGHT OF W. J. ARD

DEALER IN

DRY GOODS, BOOTS & SHOES, GENTS' FURNISHINGS,
GROCERIES, FLOUR & FEED, FURNITURE, HARDWARE,
PULPWOOD, TAN BARK AND LUMBER.

SOUTH RIVER, *Dec 5* 1917
ONTARIO

Mr *8 Baechler*

ACCOUNTS DUE MONTHLY   INTEREST AT THE RATE OF 8 PER CENT CHARGED ON OVERDUE ACCOUNTS

per mr Cottle

1917

Dec.	5	20			
		5" Cuba @	90	450
		1 Bag Y Sugar		960
		Raisins		100
		Currants		100
		57" Molasses 6½		371
		2 S. Pins		10
		1 Steamer		55
		5" B. Tea @ 50		250
		6 L Glasses 14		84
		20" R. Oats		140
		6 Matches 18		108
		1 Was. Coat		900
		1 pr Overalls		160
		1 " "		175
		2 " Long Dr 150		300
		2 " Mitts 70		140
		2 " " 75		150
		2 " Sox 40		80
		2 " " 65		130

GOOD OLD DAYS: In the good old days, a loaf of home-baked bread was something to behold. The late Mr. Thomas Wattie, top photo, holds a loaf of bread baked in an open fire in Algonquin Park. Mr. Wattie was Park Ranger from 1910 until his retirement in 1950. Lower photo shows Mr. and Mrs. Gordon Wattie of South River holding the iron pot and lid in which his father Thomas baked his own bread when stationed in the Park. The ranger's cabin which was situated at Biggar Lake near Tee Lake, has since been burned.
Photo by Lloyd Gough

Left: *W.J.Ard Statement.*

Top Right: *Amelia/Tootsie Wattie with her brother Duncan.*

Lower Right: *Tom's son Gord and wife Rhonda holding the original, heavy Wattie pot and cover. Photo Lloyd Gough.*

Tom kept up his sketching. Although it was officially a deer hunting expedition, the trio first rested on Round Lake Island where Tom painted *White Birches, Round Lake/Mud Bay, The Tent,* and *Dawn on Round Lake.* The first three he gave to Tom Wattie and the latter to Dr. McComb. The hunting took place in the country around South River, outside the park. Tom told Dr. MacCallum that on one hunting day he painted *Sand Hill on the Road to South River* and one other sketch. That same day he tramped 14 miles (22.5 km) carting his sketch box, gun, a dead fox and seven partridge, which he'd shot that day.[clxxx] It was partridge stew and bannock that evening!

Tom gave Wattie sketches when he left South River and he later sent him camping gear by train to store for him.[clxxxi] He had plans for a future Temagami trip with Tom Wattie and young Gord. By this time he trusted Wattie to such an extent that he asked him to burn certain sketches. Then he headed home to Owen Sound as his sister Minnie was visiting and he didn't want to miss that. There was no rush to return to Toronto. The Shack was empty; Franklin Carmichael had married in September.

Although Tom had his usual Shack visitors for meal times that winter, he mostly painted, snowshoed and visited with friends—including his young pal Thoreau MacDonald. Three months after he'd arrived in Toronto, he was en route back to Algonquin Park. He arrived mid-March 1916 to sketch the winter breakup of snow and ice. On April 28 he acquired a guide's licence, but in the meantime, he'd lined up a stint as a fire ranger. Tom stopped at South River on his way to the summer berth with ranger Ed Godin. There in Ard's store, Truman Kidd, the art teacher at Riverdale Collegiate in Toronto saw Tom eating a baloney sausage sandwich with biscuits and drinking a bottle of pop. Tom was at Ard's to pick up supplies. He told the chatty art teacher that he liked to get his art supplies there.[clxxxii]

Tom saw to his usual round of South River visits, fully intending to return. He never made it back. Tom's son Gord found Tom's stored items when he took over his father's Ottawa Avenue residence. He donated Tom's silk tent, fold-up cot, cast iron cooking pot and rain gear to the Algonquin Park Archives many years later. The plans for Temagami never came to be.

Postmistress Alice Smyth never married.

The Food Connection

On a visit to South River for research purposes, I was fortunate to run into local historian Keith Thornborrow. Keith generously showed me his wonderful collection of articles and photos, but best of all, he shared stories about Tom Wattie and his family. Most of the information in this chapter owes thanks to Keith and Jan Heinonen, CEO of the South River–Machar Union Library. Keith to this day remains friends with Wattie's descendants. Keith narrated the details of Tom Wattie's bread making as it had been narrated to him by Kenny Cooper (the son of Amelia "Tootsie" Wattie–Cooper) as we looked at the photo of Tom Wattie holding one of his exemplary round, sand bread loaves.

Tom Wattie first set the dough mixture in a pan in the warm sand to rise. He then punched that dough down and put it into a heavy round cast iron pan to rise several more times in the hot sand. After the final rise, he moved the pan to the cabin oven for baking. Keith has a photo taken by Lloyd Gough of Tom's son Gord and his wife Rhonda holding the original, heavy Wattie pot and its cover.

Another Wattie photo Keith had showed a box of Royal Yeast Cakes in the background. That reference started Keith and I on a discussion of yeast. Did Tom Wattie use yeast cakes for that spectacular rise in his sand bread, or was the box a reminder of a previous era, an antique of sorts?

Research on Royal Yeast Cakes showed that the yeast manufacturing plant of the Gillette Company on Front Street in Toronto fell victim to the Great Toronto Fire of 1904. The company took out an ad in the *Globe* on April 21, 1904, to reassure customers that Gillette would soon be back in operation:

> "Our entire plant (building and machinery) was totally consumed by the awful conflagration which swept part of Toronto on Tuesday night, April 19th, and we must therefore ask your indulgence for a few weeks. Fortunately we have a duplicate set of machinery stored safely in another building, and this will enable us to turn out goods within a reasonable time. Every Wholesale Grocer in the Dominion has a stock of ROYAL YEAST, GILLETTE'S LYE, MAGIC BAKING POWDER, etc., so we are hoping, by the careful use of goods now in their hands, that no one will be inconvenienced. 'Gillette's Goods Are the Best', and will be more popular than ever."

Well, I was reassured. The Gillette ad convinced me that Tom Wattie had plenty of leavening products at hand—either the Royal Yeast Cakes or the company's Magic Baking Powder. Ard's store in South River would have stocked both. Note too that the rhyming doughnut recipe in the chapter on Archie Belaney made reference to the Gillette Company's products.

I turned from yeast, next to the issue of partridge stew. Since Tom had shot seven partridge near South River, naturally I wondered about the preparation of this game. *The Toronto Cookbook* had an outline:

> "Pheasants, like all other wild birds, are not in first-class condition for cooking when freshly killed; they should be tied together by the feet and, hung in a cool, dry place until they begin to drip at the beak. Pluck and draw* the birds and singe them carefully, then put the liver of each back into the cavity; truss them with light skewers. Never stuff a pheasant under any circumstances."

> *For the uninitiated partridge preparers, one draws a bird by sticking one's forefinger up the bird's bum, rotating said finger and gently drawing out the liver and guts.

Now, on to the stewing!

Partridge Stew

Ragout of Fowl in *Mrs. Beeton's Cookery Book* from 1912 will stand in for Tom's stew as the page 190 recipe is generic.

> "Ingredients: fowl, ¼ lb. of ham or bacon cut into dice, 2 ½ oz. of butter, 1 ½ oz. of flour, 1 ½ pints of stock, 1 onion finely chopped, salt and pepper.

> Divide the fowl [in this case drawn partridge] into neat joints. Heat the butter in a stew pan, fry the pieces of fowl until nicely browned, then remove and keep it hot. Fry the onion slightly, then sprinkle in the flour, cook slowly until well browned, and add the stock. Stir until boiling, season to taste, replace the fowl, put in the ham or bacon, and cover closely. Cook very gently from 1 to 1 ¼ hours, or until the fowl is tender, then serve with the sauce strained over."

Ah, yes, and for those wondering about the firkins of butter at the South River Fall Fair. A firkin is a small wooden vessel—a barrel or cask—with a capacity of 9 gallons or 34 liters.

A firkin, photo, on wordsbybob.wordpress.com.

Ancient Scots and Irish men flavoured their butter heavily with garlic, pounded it into a wooden firkin and buried it in a nearby peat bog to take flavour. Archeological specimens have turned up centuries later as those who buried the firkin frequently forgot where they placed it. One may assume that the South River firkins of butter were fresher!

Left: *Pete Sauvé*, TUA, photo taken by Charlotte Bernardo.

Top Right: *Waiting for dinner in the cook shanty at a logging camp in the Ottawa Valley*, Harmer W. Morrell LAC-1966-033.

Lower Right: *Scotia Junction Train Station*, ca 1910, LAC-1955-078.

CHAPTER FIFTEEN

Pete Sauvé, Lumber Camp Cook, Summer 1916

"Like an army, a timber drive travels on its stomach and its camp cook is an important individual, for on his ability and trustworthiness may depend the success of the long journey from the timber limits to the mills. On this drive the cook was Pete Sauvé, who was another of those men who fell under the charm of Thomson's individuality."

Blodwen Davies, "Tom Thomson: The Story of a Man who Looked for Beauty and for Truth in the Wilderness", page 81

Pierre or Pete Sauvé was born to French–Canadian parents in Trenton, Ontario in 1880. In 1896, the Gilmour Lumber Company, headquartered in Trenton, hired the 16-year-old as a labourer. The company needed extra hands at their operation on Canoe Lake. The adventurous Pete took the train to Scotia Junction where he pivoted direction to his destination. Within a year, he was a 'cookee' helping to cook for 750 hungry lumbermen. In an undated interview by Taylor Statten[clxxiii] in the Algonquin Park Archives, Pete explained that the Gilmour brothers' scheme to take lumber south, faltered quickly. It was too costly to take the lumber, "down through Dorset. Put 'em over land there and down the Muskoka waters and into the Trent waters."[clxxiv] When the company went bankrupt, Pete worked for other lumber operations.

Top Left: Tom Thomson, *Log Jam, Sketch for "The Drive"*, Fall 1916.
Oil on composite wood-pulp board, 21.6 x 26.7 cm.
The Thomson Collection at the Art Gallery of Ontario, Toronto. © 2017.

Top Right: "Lake Trout cooking in reflector oven" Tom Thomson photo, *Bulletin 16, #14.*

Lower Right: *Out-Side-In,* photo Edward Godin, sign painted by Tom Thomson, APMA 1132.

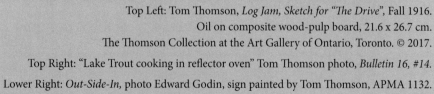

Strangely enough, even the transcripts of Pete's conversations, hold a French accent. You hear it in the story he tells the founder of Camp Ahmek, Taylor Statten, of a time in 1904 when wolves tracked him. "Well, they followed me all night … I had to rest up three times coming across the lake here. I left that place it was two thirty I left Dividing Lake, and we called it the 26 mile (42 km) jaunt, to come across to Canoe Lake here that afternoon on New Year's Day in 1905." Pete went on to say that men following him found traces that the wolves were digging right where he'd lain down during the night.[clxxxv] The Park then had a very healthy wolf population.

That same year 1905, Pete married Mary Laurentia Leduc of Ottawa. By 1916, he and Laurentia had five children. Each year, Pete left Mary Laurentia and children to make his living as a seasonal cook on lumber drives.

Pete and Tom Thomson crossed paths in June 1916 when Tom was paired as a fire ranger with Edward Godin, a 47-year-old French–Canadian from Eganville, Ontario, a community near the south eastern corner of Algonquin Park. Ed Godin wrote to Blodwen Davies in 1931 that, "Tom Thomson came to my cabin at Achray on or about the first of June having been stationed here as a Fire Ranger." [clxxxvi]

Ed and Tom passed the time amicably. They fished and chatted, sometimes about the war. Ed remembered later that, "he did not think that Canada should be involved. He [Tom] was very outspoken in his opposition to Government patronage."[clxxxvii] They spent an easy month together, as there were no fires. Ed proudly hung the sign, "Out~Side~In", which Tom painted for the ranger cabin Ed had built in previous years as a ranger at Achray. Later in the summer, they would head from Grand Lake towards the south branch of the Petawawa River (now Barron River) to do a fire circuit.

During regular fishing and painting forays in the area around Grand Lake, Tom ran into the J.R. Booth Co. lumber drive. Tom had seen many active lumber operations and the residue left behind from logging, but this was to be his first long term interaction with loggers themselves. He decided to stay with the drive. According to Blodwen Davies, Tom and lumber camp cook Pete Sauvé became good friends during the next month. "One day Thomson settled down a few feet from the cookhouse door and sketched the logs as they came tumbling through the waters at Grand Lake Dam," Pete told Taylor Statten. "He sat on the banks and stayed in this old tent for several days until he succeeded in getting that picture."

Top Left: *Life on a Lumber Raft,* Charles Stanley Reinhart, *Harper's Weekly* October 4, 1873, PD.

Centre: *J.R. Booth Cookery Raft,* photo, LAC Digital Collection, C-008405.

Top Right: Bean Hole Beans in an iron pot, PD.

Right: *Bean Hole drawing,* PD.

Left: Tom Thomson. *The Canoe,* Spring or Fall 1914. Oil on canvas, 17.3 x 25.3 cm. Gift from the J.S. McLean Collection, Toronto, 1969, Donated by the Ontario Heritage Foundation, 1988. © 2017 Art Gallery of Ontario.

Tom Thomson *Lumber Camp, Night,* 1916 oil on wood, 20.9 x 26.6 cm
Bequest of Dr. J.M. MacCallum, Toronto, 1944
National Gallery of Canada, Ottawa Photo.

found that he was a nice, a perfect, gentleman." Pete watched with professional curiosity as Tom baked trout and bass with his reflector oven, and used it to bake bannock, which he then slathered with his own homemade preserves.

The ever-generous Tom made fishing tackle for Pete. Blodwen Davies wrote that, "… he [Sauvé] took the fishing tackle Tom had made for him, regarding it as a souvenir of a brief friendship that was, somehow or other, remarkable, and he has kept it ever since."[clxxxviii] Sauvé added that Tom was, "a good fellow, who sure could paint and eat."

Although officially stationed at Achray, Tom liked the lumber camp enough to sleep and eat there. According to Pete, "he boarded with us. He had his meals with us while he was painting his pictures." Those weeks of meals exposed Tom to lumber camp cooking, centred as it was in the camboose or central fireplace. Every lumber camp had a central sandpit for the fire; even the cookhouses that were portable on boats had them. The cook lined a hole in the sand pit with rocks and started a fire over it, or he placed preheated rocks in the hole. Either way, the bake kettle was buried in the hot sand to simmer for hours. The baked fare was usually beans, molasses and salt pork.

There were other pictures Tom liked and got: pointer boats, log jams, the lumber camp at night and the alligator, a boat equipped with a cable and winch which allowed it to pull itself over land and around portages. When not dabbing paint to boards, Tom went fishing. Pete told Statten, "I went out with Tom, and went across Grand Lake to a little lake that come right into Grand Lake, White Lake. I fished there with him and I

Left: *Camboose Camp (lumbermen dancing),* photo from a painting by David. B. Keenan, AO-DBS, 1-273-1-0-30-4.

Right: From left in photo: Mark Robinson, Ernest Thompson Seton, Stuart Logan Thompson and Taylor Statten, 1922 photo by Alex Edmison, APMA 1848, – *all men played a part in Tom's life.*

The salt pork was a staple, as it was shipped in barrels and hauled in while winter roads were good. Bread was cooked in other great big iron 'bakkittles', as the loggers called them. Veteran cooks such as Pete Sauvé, used sheets of tin as a reflector to bake first class pies—as Tom did with his reflector oven. Tom would have discovered great similarities between his and Pete's cooking.

There would be more food variety if the lumber camp's supplies came from a depot farm—for example potatoes and root vegetables for stews. But no matter what, the tea kettle was always suspended from an iron cramière and the fire never went out, until the area was logged out and the camp moved.

Sauvé told Statten that after a day of painting, Tom sat and talked with the men. In the weeks he visited and stayed with the drive, Tom also watched the lumbermen play cards, fashion axe handles out of ironwood and sharpen their axe blades. The axe handle Tom carved in 1916, now part of the McMichael Canadian Art Collection, might well have been carved under the supervision of a Booth lumberman.

On a Saturday night, when a mouth organ, accordion or fiddle prompted one of the many shanty songs that all uncannily started with, "Come all ye's",[clxxxix] there would follow a rattling of the bones[cxc]—that's what the men called the clacking sound of their steps on wooden floors. Men designated as female dancers wore kerchiefs around their waists or over their heads and all stepped lively. Although not an image ever associated with Tom Thomson, I can easily imagine him in his Mackinaw jacket and toque do-si-do-ing and promenading with the best of the burly lumberjacks—a big grin plastered on his face.

After weeks of good painting and good times, Tom left. He and Ed were due for their fire ranger circuit. They turned their canoe to the south branch of the Petawawa River, intending to circle to the north branch and on to Lake Traverse (Travers). Before they left, Tom offered Pete his sketch of the log drive, but Pete had no storage space. Lumber camps were hastily torn down and set up as they moved, and he felt he couldn't take extra baggage. William Little in *The Tom Thomson Mystery* added, "All his life he [Sauvé] had regretted not buying it because he had always admired it."[cxci]

Mohawk Creek Harbour

Address all communications during the camp period to Camp Ahmek, Mowat P.O., Ont. Before and after camp, the address is 299 Queen Street West, Toronto. Phone Adelaide 0117.

TAYLOR STATTEN, Camp Director.

Speckled Beauties

Moose Crossing Lake

Page Twenty-Two

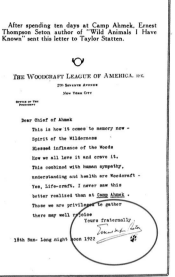

After spending ten days at Camp Ahmek, Ernest Thompson Seton author of "Wild Animals I Have Known" sent this letter to Taylor Statten.

THE WOODCRAFT LEAGUE OF AMERICA, INC.

370 SEVENTH AVENUE

NEW YORK CITY

OFFICE OF THE PRESIDENT

Dear Chief of Ahmek

This is how it comes to memory now –

Spirit of the Wilderness

Blessed influence of the Woods

How we all love it and crave it.

This combined with human sympathy,

understanding and health are Woodcraft –

Yes, Life-craft. I never saw this

better realized than at Camp Ahmek.

Those we are privileged to gather

there may well rejoice

Yours fraternally,

18th Sun- Long night noon 1922

Page Twenty-Three

TESTIMONIAL DINNER

to

CHUBBY

(ALIAS GEORGE W. CHUBB)

by

THE AHMEK OLDER GUARD (1921-1929)

Top Left: *Testimonial Dinner to Chubby, booklet,* TUA, pp 22-23 with letter by Ernest Thompson Seton.

Right: *"Chubby" George W. Chubb,* booklet cover, Alex Edmison Fonds, TUA. Tom gave George W. Chubb the painting *Melting Snow,* Winter 1914–1915.

Lower Left: Pete Sauvé wearing chef hat in centre", *Camp Ahmek,* booklet, TUA.

Cranberry Marsh and Hill, 1916, Tom Thomson, oil, in Art Gallery of Hamilton, Gallery purchase, 1953.

Tom and Ed Godin canoed through the stunningly high Petawawa Gorges to Lake Traverse just as planned. By October 4, Tom ended up in Basin Depot. He hit the cranberry harvesting season and boxed a store of them to make spiced cranberry sauces and cranberry jam back at The Shack. He shipped the boxes from Achray by CN rail. He complained to his father in a January 23, 1917 letter that, "I think they are charging too much …."

It's possible Tom and Pete saw one another again at Canoe Lake in 1917. Shortly after Tom and Pete met at Grand Lake, Pete came to be a cook on Canoe Lake. He explained to Taylor Statten, "I was cooking for a bunch of firefighters. Then, in with J.R. Booth and we were called upon to then go and fight this bush fire. Well, when they came out, Chubby[cxcii] was looking for, well, a cook. I came down here then and cooked one day. I went down to Ottawa and they sent back for me."

Michigan Logging Camp, Bay City, Michigan, photo, grisdalefamily.wordpress.com.

News of Pete Sauvé resurfaced in 1956 when Judge William Little assembled a three man crew to find and dig up Tom Thomson's remains, which he believed were in the Mowat Cemetery and not in the family plot at Leith. Judge Little said, "We met in the kitchen in back of Ahmek's great dining hall, where Pete Sauvé was serving breakfast to the maintenance staff of the camp." At that point, the good-natured Pete Sauvé had become an institution at Camp Ahmek, a summer camp for boys that had once been visited by Ernest Thompson Seton. By the 1950s Sauvé had rung the dining room bell at the camp for decades. Algonquin Park historian Audrey Sanders writes, "His [Sauvé's] good-natured disposition, and his ability to make first-class pies, … made him a favourite with staff and campers alike."[cxciii]

Judge Little and his gravediggers returned to the camp, buzzing with news of a spectacular find they'd made at Mowat Cemetery. They believed they'd found the skull of Tom Thomson. And thus, Pete Sauvé who'd sat beside his friend Tom in a canoe 40 years before and who chatted with him by firelight, was there when the spirit of Tom Thomson entered the Camp Ahmek dining room.

The Food Connection

Before we get to what Tom and Pete might have cooked, here's Charles Ellis' account of the amount of food that 55 men consumed in a Michigan lumber camp in 1885. Lumberjacks sure could eat!

"Our fifty-five men have consumed in twenty weeks the following quantities of first class provisions:

30 bbls. (barrels) flour	500 lbs. tea
22 bbls. pork (salt)	4,000 lbs. fresh meat
15 bbls. beef	150 lbs. baking powder
1,200 lbs. lard	300 bu (bushels) potatoes
400 lbs. butter	30 bu. beans
1,200 lbs. sugar	150 gals. (gallons) molasses

8 bbls. crackers (hardtack)

6,000 pickles

together with cabbage, onions, turnips, etc. This represents a great deal of eating, but the work done will balance it off."

Ellis published this table of lumber camp consumption in *The Chicago Current* in an article titled "Among the Michigan Pines". Pete Sauvé had his work cut out for him on the Booth Lumber Drive.

Today we get pork and beans in a can. In Tom's day, the process of getting a gut-filling pot of baked beans for hungry lumberjacks or campers, was a much longer process. The *Toronto (Queen City of Canada) Cookbook* has a standard kitchen version. Tom could have soaked his beans overnight in lake water and buried his Dutch oven in the sand, the way Pete Sauvé would have done. Audrey Sanders in *The Algonquin Story* writes that, "nothing nowadays can compare with beans baked in the sand for a long period of time, or with bread cooked in the same manner in the great iron 'bakkittles'".[cxciv]

Pork and Beans

"Put one pound of beans to soak overnight, boil in morning till soft, put into baking pan two tablespoons of molasses, one small onion, one pound fat, pickled pork and a dash of pepper; cover with water, put in a moderate oven and bake all day, adding a cup of water every little while to keep from burning."

Vinegar Pie
a traditional logging camp recipe

1 ¼ cup granulated sugar, 1 ½ cups boiling water, $\frac{1}{3}$ cup vinegar, $\frac{1}{3}$ cup corn starch, dash of nutmeg, 3 eggs, 1 tablespoon butter, baked 9" pie shell.

Separate eggs and beat yolks together. Stir together the first five ingredients and cook until clear and thick. Stir half the mixture into beaten egg yolks; add mixture to remaining mix in saucepan and stir until combined; let rest off stove for one minute. Stir in a tablespoon of butter until melted. Pour into a baked pie shell.

And now for something every cook on a large scale appreciates: a recipe for leftovers from *Fancy Meats in Newest Dishes*.

"Scrapple"

7 cups of water,

2 ½ cups cornmeal,

3 teaspoons salt,

2 cups chopped meat.

Make a mush of cornmeal. Add meat and cook two to three hours in a double boiler or fireless cooker. Put in a mold to cool. Slice and sauté in hot fat. Crackling from the rendering may be used in place of meat."

I had difficulty finding period recipes for cranberries dating to Tom's time. Well, that's not quite true. Mrs. J. Hoodless, the President of Domestic Science in Hamilton, Ontario published a very basic recipe in 1898 in *Public School Domestic Science.*

Cranberries

"Ingredients 1 pint of cranberries,
1 cup of sugar and 1 cup of water.

"Eatmor Cranberries", *Good Housekeeping,* November, 1926, PD.

Instructions. Put the cranberries in a granite saucepan, the sugar, water. After they begin to boil cook 10 minutes, closely covered. (this may be pressed through a sieve while hot, removing the skins, if desired for a mould."

Eatmor Cranberries had a simple recipe that seemed Shack-appropriate and basically no different than Mrs. Hoodless' version.

Recipes for Eatmor Fresh Cranberries, pamphlet, *Good Housekeeping* 1951.

Eatmor Cranberries, *Good Housekeeping*, November, 1926
"All you need: —2 cups water, 1 ½ to 2 cups sugar, 1 lb. (4 cups) cranberries.

All you need to do: Boil sugar and water together for five minutes; add the cranberries and boil without stirring (five minutes is usually sufficient) until all the skins are broken. Remove from the fire when popping stops."

The 1926 advertisement did, however provide some extra ideas. It notes that Cranberry Sauce makes a tasty filling for pies, tarts, puddings and shortcakes and that jelly may be put up in glass jars for future use. A later *Recipes for Eatmor Fresh Cranberries* booklet published in 1951 has variants for the Eatmor product: Cranberry Ambrosia, Minted Cranberry Sauce, Cranberry Apricot Delight, Cranberry Chiquita and Cranberry-Ruby Pears. They all sound delicious and they're very simple for the kitchen but not the camp. Here are two Tom might have tried in The Shack:

"**Minted Cranberry Sauce**. Stir in teaspoon chopped fresh mint or few drops mint extract for Minted Cranberry Sauce."

"**Cranberry Chiquita.** Fold in 3 bananas cut in ½ inch slices for Cranberry Chiquita."

Basically it's easy to add anything to cranberries: oranges, apples, apricots. No wonder Tom had cranberries shipped from up north.

South River, photo, Angie Littlefield.

Acknowledgements

I consulted many helpful librarians and archivists during long years of research. The list below identifies the institutions and, where possible, the persons who helped dig for details on Tom Thomson and period cooking. The work on Tom's less documented friends, had to be even more rigorous as these individuals left fainter traces in history.

Thanks to:

Edward Taylor Research Library and Archives and Art Gallery of Ontario, **Dr. Amy Furness** and **Tracy Mallon-Jensen**; Thomas Fisher Rare Book Library, **Liztopher Rolf**; Guelph University Culinary Archives, **Melissa McAfee**; Trent University Library, Alex Edmison Fonds; Algonquin Park Archives, **Ron Tozer** and **Trina Chatelain**; South River historian **Keith Thornborrow**, South River–Machar Union Public Library, **Jan Heinonen**; McMichael Canadian Art Collection, **Alexandra Cousins** and Archives **Linda Morita**; City of Sheffield Archives, **Tim Knebel**; Muskoka Heritage Place, **Sara White**; Huntsville Public Library, **Richard Harwood, Courtney LeGros** and **Deborah Duce;** Comber and District Historical Society Museum, **Mark McKinlay**; Monroe County Historical Museum, **Caitlyn Riehle**; City of Toronto Archives; Toronto Reference Library; Archives of Ontario, Donald B. Smith fonds; Tom Thomson Memorial Gallery, **David Huff**; Grey Roots Museum and Archives, **Karin Noble** and **Kate Jackson;** Glenbow Archives, **Lynette Walton**; Library and Archives Canada, Tom Thomson Collection; The National Gallery, Canada, **Bianca Fortier** and **Veronique Malouin;** Alpena County Library, Michigan, **Marlo Broad;** Library and Information Services University Health Network, **Ani Orchanian-Cheff**; Arts and Letters Club, **Scott James**; Canadian War Museum, **Susan Ross**; Beaverbrook Art Gallery, **Sarah Dick**; Art Gallery of Hamilton, **Christine Braun**; Winnipeg Art Gallery, **Nicole Fletcher**; Whyte Museum of the Canadian Rockies, **Elizabeth Kundert-Cameron**; OENO Gallery, **Carlyn Moulton**.

Certain individuals stand out in their support of this project. White Pine Pictures researchers Rebecca Middleton and Nancy Lang generously shared information and leads and Rebecca stepped up as well to do the final and meticulous copy editing. Thomson/Matheson descendants provided detailed information and photos. They even wrote commentary on drafts of my writing. My thanks to: David, Helen and Tim Young, Kay Morrison, Margaret McLaughlin and David Thomson. Descendants of friends and neighbours of Tom Thomson were equally generous with family stories. Thanks to Paul Simon, David and Gail Ainslie, Marcia Armstrong and Jaffray Rutherford. You sparked interesting research. Janet Cauffiel, a descendant of Arthur Lismer, Sylvia Telford of the Hayhursts of Canoe Lake and Paul Gauthier, son of Joachim Gauthier, a friend of Franklin Carmichael, were equally generous with access to wonderful photos and works. Carlyn Moulton of OENO Gallery and John Libby of the John A. Libby Gallery generously enabled the use of other images. Thank you to Carolyn Lomax for preliminary editing. I also value the support of graphic designer Andrea Ketelaars.

Additionally, I owe a debt those who researched and wrote about Tom Thomson before me. Had Blodwen Davies not interviewed Tom Thomson family and friends, it would have been much more difficult to delve into the details of his life. The works of art historians contributed valuable leads about Tom's life: Joan Murray, Dennis Reid, Charles Hill and Ross King, to name just a few. Additionally the internet made available wonderful resources such as *Tom Thomson Catalogue Raisonné, The West Wind* and *Death on a Painted Lake.* When it came down to the nitty-gritty, niche researchers and ancestry.ca came through. John Sabean knew the Thomson family history in Claremont; Neil Lehto knew Seattle; David and Gail Ainslie opened up Comber; Keith Thornborrow honed in on South River; ancestry.ca supplied the background for Tom's landlords.

I experienced another substantial level of support from Charles Hill and Debby Hay. Charles went over my manuscript helping me to buckle down to details and Debby stimulated valuable new angles in the research. Friends Ruth Abernethy, Ruth Redelmeier, Robbie Lavack and Amanda Hale were rocks of support. My friend Linda Neilly supported me even further, accompanying me on research trips to South River and Comber.

Needless to say, the book's designer Mary Cook was and is astounding. She launched herself into this daunting project with inspirational enthusiasm and energy. Her keen eye, graphic talents and no nonsense work ethic are the foundation of this book. Thank you Mary!!

Finally, I started research into Tom Thomson and his heritage 12 years ago when the AGO's Chief Curator Dennis Reid allowed The Durham West Arts Centre (a tiny start-up gallery) to participate in the provincial G7 Exhibition. When The Tom Thomson Gallery in Owen Sound generously agreed to loan DWAC original Tom Thomson works for an exhibition, well, the game was afoot!

My husband David, our daughter Jennifer, her husband Oscar and the grandgirls Charlotte and Samantha have now lived through 12 years with Tom and I.

I dedicate this labour of love to them.

Bibliography for *Tom Thomson's: Fine Kettle of Friends*

Addison, Ottelyn, *Early Days in Algonquin Park,* Toronto, McGraw-Hill Ryerson, 1974

Addison, Ottelyn and Elizabeth Harwood, *Tom Thomson: The Algonquin Years,* Toronto, Ryerson Press, 1969

Anahareo, *Devil in Deerskins: My Life with Grey Owl,* Toronto, Paperjacks, 1972

Ancestry.ca: Families of Captain John Thomas Burke, Joseph Robert Watson and Thursa Heywood Watson, William Muir Twaddle (later Tweedale), Janet Gibson Henry, Esther Varty Plewes, Annie Ainslie, Luty James Thomson, Henry, Louisa, Minnie and Ralph Thomson, Pete Sauvé

Armitage, Andrew, *Vanishing: Lost Places in Grey and Bruce,* Owen Sound, Ginger Press, 2015

Bice, Megan, *Light & Shadow: The work of Franklin Carmichael,* Kleinburg, McMichael Canadian Art Collection, 1990

Billinghurst, Jane, *The Many Faces of Archie Belaney, Grey Owl,* Vancouver, Grey Stone Books/Douglas & McIntyre, 1999

Boyanoski, Christine and John Hartman, *W.J. Wood: paintings and graphics,* Toronto, Art Gallery of Ontario, 1983

Boyer, Patrick J., *A Passion for Justice: The Legacy of James Chalmers McRuer,* Toronto, Dundurn Press, 2008

Bradburn, Jamie, "Vintage Toronto Ads: Brown Betty Tea Rooms", *torontoist.com*, January 7, 2015

"Byron Harmon Fonds", *Whyte Museum of the Canadian Rockies, Archives and Library,* albertaonrecord.ca/byron-harmon-fonds-2

Canada Food Board, *Fancy Meats in Newest Dishes,* Ottawa, Canada Food Board, 1918

Casas, Teresa, "head garnish", *Back to the Park,* April 19, 2014. Backtothepark.wordpress.com

Davies, Blodwen, *Tom Thomson: The Story of a Man who Looked for Beauty and for Truth in the Wilderness,* Vancouver, Mitchell Press, 1967

Death on a Painted Lake: The Tom Thomson Tragedy, Website: *canadianmysteries.ca/sites/thomson/home/indexen.html*

Dickson, Lovat, *Wilderness Man: The Strange Story of Grey Owl,* Toronto, Macmillan Co., 1973

Department of Marine and Fisheries, *Eat More Fish: recipes and hints for the cook,* Ottawa, 1921

Duval, Paul, "Art Memorial to a 'Vital Period'", *Telegram,* September 1, 1962

Edison, Margaret, *Thoreau MacDonald: a catalogue of design and illustration,* Toronto, University of Toronto Press, 1973

Elliott, James, "Artist's brush lacked the color in his life", *Windsor Star,* May 9, 1981

Ellis, Charles, "Among the Michigan Pine", *The Chicago Current,* 1885

Farr, Dorothy M., *J.W. Beatty 1869–1941,* Kingston, Agnes Etherington Art Centre, 1981

Frayne, Trent, "The Rebel Painter of the Pine Woods", *Maclean's Magazine,* July 1, 1953

Frederick S. Challener Collection, Toronto, Art Gallery of Ontario, 1955 (files: J.W. Beatty, J.E.H. MacDonald, Tom Thomson, Albert Robson, Franklin Carmichael, William Cruikshank, Owen Staples, Tom McLean, John Thomas Rolph, Albert Curtis Williamson) prepared by Amy Marshall, 2004

Groves, Naomi Jackson, *A.Y.'s Canada*, Toronto, Clarke, Irwin & Co., 1968

Hammond, Susan and John Sabean ed., *A Boy All Spirit: Thoreau MacDonald in the 1920s,* Toronto, Penumbra Press, 2003

Hertzberg, Louise, *A Pocketful of Galls: William Brodie and the Natural History Society of Toronto,* Louise Hertzberg, 1986

Hicks, Kathleen A., *Meadowvale: Mills to Millenium,* Mississauga, Friends of the Mississauga Library System, 2004

Hoodless, Mrs. J., *Public School Domestic Science,* Toronto, Copp, Clark, 1898

Hoover, Dorothy, *J.W. Beatty,* Toronto, Ryerson Press, 1948

Housser, F.B., *Canadian Art Movement: Story of the Group of Seven,* Toronto, Macmillan Co, 1926

Jackson, A.Y., *A Painter's Country,* Canada, Clarke, Irwin and Co., 1958

Jaeger, Ellsworth, *Wildwood Wisdom,* New York, Scribner, 1945

Kikauka, Gita Marie, "Frederick Stanley Haines: A Good Life Lived, an Enduring Legacy Left", *The Frederick S. Haines Commemorative Exhibition,* Meaford, 2010

King, Ross, *Defiant Spirits: The Modernist Revolution of the Group of Seven,* Kleinburg, McMichael Canadian Art Collection/Douglas & McIntyre, 2010

KLIM, Powdered Whole Milk, *Easy Recipes For Camp and Kitchen,* Canada, nd

Lehto, Neil, *Algonquin Elegy: Tom Thomson's Last Spring,* I-universe, 2005. Website: algonquinelegy.com/index.html

Little, William T., *The Tom Thomson Mystery,* Toronto, Mc-Graw-Hill, 1970

Littlefield, A., *The Thomsons of Durham: Tom Thomson's Family Heritage,* Pickering, Durham West Arts Centre, 2005
   Ibid, *Tom Thomson's Toronto Neighbourhoods,* angielittlefield.com, 2010

   Ibid, *Two of the Talented Thomsons: George Thomson, Margaret Thomson,* Toronto, John A. Libby Fine Art, 2006

Litvak, Marilyn, *Edward James Lennox "builder of Toronto",* Toronto, Dundurn Press, 1995

Luttrell, Julia, "Grey Owl – Anatomy of a Myth", *Northern Stories,* northernontario.org/NorthernStories/GreyOwlJL.htm

MacDonald, Thoreau, *Notebooks,* Ontario, Penumbra Press, 1980
   Ibid, *The Group of Seven,* Toronto, Ryerson Press, 1944

Mackey, Doug, "Heritage Perspectives" (assorted), pastforward.ca
   Ibid, *Voices from the past: Heritage perspectives 1,* Toronto, Past Forward Heritage, 2010

Mastin, Catharine M., *Portrait of a Spiritualist: Franklin Carmichael and the National Gallery Collection,* Ottawa, National Gallery, 2001

McLeish, John A.B., *September gale; a study of Arthur Lismer and the Group of Seven,* Toronto, J.M. Dent, 1955

Moments in History: 1892–1992, South River, Grace Anglican Church & South River Community, 1992

Mrs. Beeton's Cookery Book, London and Melbourne, Ward, Lock & Co., 1912

Murray, Joan, *The Best of Tom Thomson,* Edmonton, Hurtig Publishers, 1986
   Ibid, *Tom Thomson: Catalogue Raisonné,* tomthomson-catalogue.org

   Ibid, *Tom Thomson: design for a Canadian hero,* Toronto, Dundurn Press, 1998

   Ibid, *Tom Thomson: the last spring*, Toronto, Dundurn Press, 1994

   Ibid, *Tom Thomson: Trees,* Toronto, McArthur & Company, 1999

Neal, Bill, *Bill Neal's Southern Cooking,* North Carolina, University of North Carolina Press, 1989

Neil, E. *Every-Day Cook Book: Encyclopedia of Practical Recipes,* Chicago, Regan Printing House, 1892

Ontario Society of Artists, *Catalogue of the second exhibition of the Toronto Architectural Eighteen Club,* Toronto, Ontario Society of Artists' Galleries, May 19th to May 31st, 1902

Owl, Grey, *Men of the Last Frontier,* Toronto, Dundurn Press, 2011

Pink, Hal, *Bill Guppy king of the woodsmen, life-long friend and tutor of "Grey Owl",* London and Melbourne, Hutchinson & Co., 1940, ourroots.ca/e/page.aspx?id=893627

Powell, E.J., *The Toronto, Queen City of Canada, cook book,* Toronto, 1915

Recipes for Eatmor Fresh Cranberries, New York, 1951

Recipes from Muskoka, The Parish Guild of All Saints Anglican Church, Huntsville, 1951

Reed, Nathaneal, *Goodbyes Along The Way: The People and Stories of Mattagami First Nations*, Newcastle, Penumbra, 2012

Reid, Dennis and Charles Hill, *Tom Thomson,* Vancouver/Toronto, Douglas & McIntyre, 2002

Reid, Dennis, "Photographs by Tom Thomson", *Bulletin 16,* 1970, gallery.ca/bulletin/num16/reid1.html

   Ibid, *Tom Thomson: The Jack Pine,* Ottawa, The National Gallery of Canada, 1975

Reliable Recipes: compiled by Mrs. J. Wilkinson, Mrs. M. Staples, Mrs. W. Wilkinson, Mrs. J. MacLennan, Aberdeen, Saskatchewan, Talent Money for Ladies' Aid, United Church, 1927

Research Committee of Muskoka Pioneer Village, *Huntsville: pictures from the past,* Boston Mills Press, 1997

Rhodes, Susie Root and Grace Porter Hopkins, eds., *The Economy Administration Cook Book,* Hammond, IN, W.B. Conkey Co., 1913

Robson, Albert H. *Tom Thomson,* Toronto, Ryerson Press, 1937

   Ibid, Albert H., *J.E.H. MacDonald,* Toronto, Ryerson Press, 1937

Ross, Allan H., *Reminiscences of North Sydenham: An Historical Sketch of Annan and Leith,* Owen Sound, Richardson, Bond & Wright, 1924

Saunders, Audrey, *Algonquin Story,* Toronto, Department of Lands and Forests, 1947

Seneca (Henry H. Soule), *Canoe and Camp Cookery: A Practical Cook Book for Canoeists, Corinthian Sailors and Outers,* New York, Forest and stream publishing co.,1885

Shaw, Bernard S., "Medicare in Algonquin Park", *The Country Connections Magazine*, Issue 38, Winter 2002

Smith, Donald B., *From the Land of Shadows: the Making of Grey Owl,* Saskatoon, Western Prairie Books, 1990

Staples, Owen, "He was a Pioneer in Art, Friend Says of J.W. Beatty", *Toronto Telegram,* October 9, 1941

Stuart Logan Thompson Fonds, Royal Ontario Museum Archives, Toronto, from 1902–1961

The Comber and District Historical Society, *Comber Through the Years,* Leamington, The Comber & District Historical Society Museum, 2009

The Forester, Huntsville, Canadian Community Digital Archives, communitydigitalarchives.com

The Home Cook Book: compiled by ladies of Toronto and chief cities and town in Canada, Toronto, Hunter-Rose Co., 1920s

The Last Best West, Ottawa, 1907, Library and Archives Canada, data2.archives.ca/ap/c/c030621.jpg

Thom, Ian, "Franklin Carmichael", *Franklin Carmichael: Prints/Gravures,* Kleinburg, McMichael Canadian Art Collection and Mrs. Mary Mastin, 1984

Thompson, Stuart L., "Letter to Alan Jarvis, Director of the National Gallery of Canada, February 4, 1956", *Tom Thomson: Catalogue Raisonné, (*presently unlocated by the Library and Archives of the National Gallery of Canada)

Tippett, Maria *Stormy Weather: F.H. Varley a Biography,* Toronto, McClelland and Stewart, 1998

Town, Harold and David P. Silcox, *Tom Thomson: The Silence and the Storm,* Toronto, McClelland and Steward, 1977

Waddington, Jim and Sue Waddington, *In the Footsteps of the Group of Seven,* Sudbury, Goose Lane Editions, 2013

Walton, Izaak, *The Compleat Angler,* Ontario, Ecco Press/Penguin, 1995. First published London, Marriot, 1653

Warner, E., *Purity Flour Cookbook,* Toronto, Domestic Science Department of the MacDonald Institute, 1917

West Wind: The Vision of Tom Thomson, tomthomsonart.ca

W. J. Wood Collection, Art Gallery of Ontario, 2004 (prepared by Amy Marshall)

endnotes

[i] Minnie Thomson Henry to Blodwen Davies, February 2, 1931, "I can see him first as a small boy with a string of fish caught in the creek where he would clean and smoke in a piece of stove pipe, and I still remember how delicious they were." *West Wind* website.

[ii] A. Armitage, "Dock a relic of busy village", *The Sun Times*, August 7, 2009, "The dock was a focal point for Leith. From the roof of the cattle and wood sheds, some 18 feet [5.5 metres] above the water, young men proving their diving bravery. Not only was it an excellent place from which to fish, Ainslie's Wharf was also a choice place to stroll on a summer evening, watching the sunset over the distant escarpment."

[iii] O. Addison and E. Harwood, *Tom Thomson: The Algonquin Years*, p 19, "In an 18 foot [5.5 metres] rowboat they would start out early in the morning for the shoals near Owen Sound. By evening, if the fish continued biting, John Thomson would say, 'Let's just have another row around.' The other boys would grumble but Tom never seemed to mind."

[iv] Ibid p 4, "His love of music gave him an interest in concerts, particularly those of the Mendelssohn Choir in Toronto; his brother Fraser recalled his, 'whistling the tunes all the way home.'"

[v] Louisa Thomson also appears as Louise Thomson. On her marriage certificate registered May 29, 1907, she appears as Louisa.

[vi] John Thomson's parents were Thomas "Tam" Thomson (1806–1875) and Elizabeth Brodie Thomson (1812–1874); their farm consisted of the northeast quarter of Lots 13 and 14 in Concession A, Pickering Township. Information from historian John Sabean.

[vii] "The Toronto and Sydenham road is a diagonal line, running N.W. and S.E., nearly from corner to corner of the County of Grey. It was intended to afford as direct communication as possible, between Sydenham (Owen Sound), and Toronto-hence the name.... It was surveyed in 1848." *Directory of the County of Grey for 1864–6.* Available on ancestry.com.

[viii] Wilson Buzza, "Lot 36, Concession A, Sydenham Township", Annan Women's Institute, *Tweedsmuir History*, April 1980, p 59 (Grey Roots Museum and Archive).

[ix] Louisa Thomson Henry Letter to Blodwen Davies, March 11, 1931, "Letters", *West Wind website*, "Finally the Dr. told Mother to keep him out of school for a year and let him roam the woods with a shotgun, which he did, wearing an old felt hat which he soaked with water and shaped to a point over a broom handle, decorated with squirrel tails and wild flowers. In this way he became an expert with the shotgun and rifle, to his own delight and Mother's despair."

[x] Allan Ross Letter to Blodwen Davies, June 11, 1930, *Reminiscences of North Sydenham*, p 270.

[xi] Op cit, "I am not very clear on this point, but think Tom's share when he reached 21 was something like $1800 or $2000". Ross King, *Defiant Spirits,* p 9 works this out to be enough to build a house in Toronto in 1898.

xii The Annie Mitchell Rutherford Diary of 1894 is held by Rutherford family descendants. Entries from the first two months: "January 4, 1894, Louisa Thomson here for tea; January 7, Mrs. Thomson here; January 19, Mac & I at Mr. Thomsons; February 15, I was up at Mr Thomsons; February 16, Mr & Mrs Thomson & Miss Mathison here in the evening ...."

xiii Ibid, "Monday 3 [September] Mr. Thomson's had the threshing machine. Very warm." Mrs. Rutherford had already mentioned that they, the Juylians, McKeens, Waddells, Souters and Taylors had the threshing machine.

xiv There were also brothers: Alexander and Angus Matheson. See, Angie Littlefield *The Thomsons of Durham: Tom Thomson's Family Heritage.*

xv James Thomson lived for only 10 months, September 24, 1882 to July 11, 1883.

xvi Minnie Thomson Henry to Blodwen Davies, February 2, 1931, on the *West Wind* website.

xvii According to Marg McLaughlin, granddaughter of May Catherine Gilchrist, her grandmother was originally named Katie May Gilchrist, after her mother Katie Matheson Tripp but altered her name to May Catherine.

xviii Tom Thomson letter to Elizabeth Harkness in 1904, on the *West Wind* website.

xix Minnie Thomson Henry, letter to Blodwen Davies, February 2, 1931, *West Wind* website.

xx Photos of Jessie's teaching days are in the Jessie Harkness Collection at wellesleyhistory.org/jessie-harkness-collection.html.

xxi Elizabeth's son was Norman Douglas Harkness and her grandson was Ralph Norman Harkness.

xxii Helen Young is the granddaughter of Elizabeth Thomson-Harkness.

xxiii Ralph Norman Harkness, letter to John Libby Fine Arts, August 26, 2008.

xxiv David Ainslie is the grandson of Marcia and W.J. Ainslie who were Gladys Ainslie's uncle and aunt.

xxv Francis R. McLaren, who had taught at the Chatham Business School, opened a business school with George Thomson in Seattle. By 1908 he had moved to Owen Sound with his wife Isabel and two children.

xxvi Letty James also appears as Luty James on documents but it is the same person.

xxvii Ancestry.ca records February 28, 1907 as the date of the Louisa Thomson – James Henry marriage but the registration date is May 29, 1907 in Owen Sound.

xxviii National Gallery of Canada description: sketchbook containing 22 drawings in graphite on 43 sheets of wove paper, bound in leather covers. Dimensions: 13.0 x 20.9 cm.

xxix Joan Murray remarks, "Decorative Landscape, Quotation from Henry van Dyke", *Catalogue Raisonné* website.

xxx "List of Artworks by or Attributed to Tom Thomson", *The Tom Thomson Collection Accession No. 1995-133*, Archives of Canada, p 11.

xxxi Tom Thomson letter to his father, January 23, 1917, on the *West Wind* website.

xxxii The 159th (1st Algonquins) Battalion CEF was a unit of the Canadian Expeditionary Force during WWI. The unit, based in Haileybury, started recruiting in late 1915 in Nipissing and

Sudbury. William "Bill" Guppy who in a later chapter plays a role in Archie Belaney's life, was the mascot handler for the Algonquins.

xxxiii Blodwen Davies, *Tom Thomson,* p 88.

xxxiv Allan Ross, letter to Blodwen Davies, June 11, 1930, *Reminiscences of North Sydenham,* p 271.

xxxv Ralph Thomson arrived in Seattle January 11, 1902.

xxxvi I have been unable to locate the source for Jaffray Rutherford's photocopy of a newspaper photo. Titled, "A Group of Grey County Old Boys Who Reside in Seattle, Washington", the photo shows 11 men including: Ralph, Henry, George and Tom Thomson as well as Horace Rutherford, William Henry and Allan Ross.

xxxvii A. Littlefield, *Two of the Talented Thomsons,* p 2, "by 1903 it was known as the Acme Business School. George [Thomson] was instructor and partner in this new business and at various points his brothers Ralph, Henry and Tom studied there."

xxxviii Neil Lehto, *Algonquin Elegy,* p 78. Lehto provides well researched, accurate details in his historical fiction.

xxxix The website skagitriverjournal.com/WA/Snoh/Library/Lambert/Alice1-Bio1.html cites Joan Murray's possession of the letters.

xl From a 1971 interview of Alice Elinor Lambert conducted by Joan Murray and recorded on the algonquineleigy.com website by Neil J. Lehto.

xli tomthomsonlegacy.ca/biography/first-known-landscape-oil-1904 on West Wind website.

xlii The provenance of this early oil of Puget Sound goes from Alice Elinor Lambert to a friend she makes later in her life, Martha Edmonds.

xliii Tom gifted *Puget Sound* to boarder Alice Elinor Lambert.

xliv The Telford farm, Lot 36, Concession B, abutted Rose Hill farm on the east side. Col. James Pattison Telford (1839–1933) a blacksmith by trade, was commissioned a Lieutenant in the Leith Rifles in 1863 and served with this unit during the Fenaid Raid of 1866. From 1894–1900 he commanded the 31st Grey Regiment. The Colonel and John Thomson were neighbours, fishing buddies and very good friends the whole time Tom Thomson was growing up. James' brother William, who Tom also knew, was a member of parliament from 1904–1908.

xlv According to Joan Murray's Chronology in *Tom Thomson* (edited by Dennis Reid), Tom worked for Maring and Ladd (later Maring and Blake), and the Seattle Engraving Company.

xlvi Sara's grave marker is inscribed, Sara T. Heyworth, July 2, 1861–December 7, 1927.

xlvii Louisa Henry letter cited above, "At one place where he had a room in Toronto he had a card tacked up on the outside of the door with skull and crossbones and 'The Devil's Den' written below it."

xlviii *The Thomsons of Durham: Tom Thomson's Family Heritage* (Durham West Arts Centre, 2005) tells the story of Tam Thomson and Elizabeth Brodie Thomson.

xlix Interestingly, Dr. James MacCallum removed the lenses from Dr. Brodie's eyes to restore a minute amount of vision.

l Louise Herzberg *A Pocketful of Galls,* p 25.

li Allan Ross letter to Blodwen Davies, June 11, 1930 on *West Wind website.*

liii John McRuer was a lifelong Mason achieving the status of a 'master' in Freemason's Unity Lodge, No. 376, Huntsville. The lawyer Samuel A. Hutcheson was a master of the same lodge.

liv S. Bernard Shaw, "Medicare in Algonquin Park", *The Country Connections Magazine,* Issue 38, Winter 2002.

lv On the *Catalogue Raisonné* website, Joan Murray cites Judge S.A. Hutchinson as owner of *The Banks of the River.* Judge S.A. Hutchinson was, in fact, Samuel Albert(us) Hutcheson, or "Bert". Hutcheson, a Huntsville lawyer from 1900–1911 and a master in Unity Lodge in 1908, Hutcheson was friends with fellow mason Dr. John McRuer and Tom accompanied them on hunting expeditions. John's brother, James McRuer, articled with "Bert" before he left for Swift Current. S.A. Hutcheson ended up as a District Judge in Saskatchewan.

lvi Stuart Logan Thompson was the son of Ernest Seton's older brother William Snowden Thompson. Stuart was born in Toronto in 1885; he was a naturalist who, like Dr. Brodie, gathered specimens. The ROM holds 493 bird specimens Thompson gathered. The Stuart Thompson Fonds at University of Toronto Libraries contains 28 journals of bird observation, the earliest from January 25, 1902.

lvii After Long's death Woodlawn was demolished to make way for Jarvis Collegiate.

lviii From the obituary of Elizabeth McCarnen's mother Mary Ann McCarnen which appeared in the *Northern Gazette,* May 4, 1910 p 8. I saw a copy of the obituary in the collection of her grandnephew, Paul Simon.

lix Stories of Elizabeth McCarnen and Tom Thomson were kept alive by her niece Rita Tomlinson who was raised by Elizabeth in Toronto. Rita's descendants still tell those stories.

lxxxvii "He [Captain John T. Burke] moved here from Penetang,

lx Trent Frayne described a woman who did all these things with Tom.

lxi Pat Hope, "A Place of Their Own: Medicine – 2" dated 29 March 1995 in a vertical file in the Huntsville Public Library, Muskoka Room.

lxii Stuart Logan Thompson Letter to Alan Jarvis, February 4, 1956 on the *Catalogue Raisonné website,* "Three Missing Documents recorded in the 1970s".

lxiii Tom's pencil sketches of his brother George Thomson show George with slicked back hair parted in the middle—very unlike the portrait of the man with a mustache who has bushy hair (and was likely Ernest Thompson Seton).

lxiv *The Forester* is online at *Canadian Community Digital Archives website communitydigitalarchives.com.*

lxv John McRuer and Edythe Bullock's marriage details are on Ancestry.ca.

lxvi Tom left his mandolin at Pembroke Street and eventually it made its way to the McMichael Canadian Collection Archive.

lxvii Patrick Boyer, "McRuer in Muskoka*", Muskoka Times*, November 2, 1997, p 2. Muskoka Room, Huntsville Library.

lxviii William Smithson Broadhead's correspondence is in the Sheffield Libraries, Archives and Information.

lxx The *City of Toronto Directory* identifies William Henry MacDonald (1850–1936), cabinet maker, as the owner of 475 Quebec Avenue in 1908. According to John Sabean, editor of *A Boy All Spirit,* p 19, the house at 475 was later renumbered to 105 Quebec Avenue.

lxxi John Sabean, editor, *A Boy All Spirit: Thoreau MacDonald in the 1920s*, p 19. "In his earliest years, MacDonald lived with his parents in a rented cottage at 572 Quebec Ave, about a half-mile north of High Park. ... In December 1903, however, he went to London, England, to join the Carlton Studio Designers and Illustrators …Late in 1907, J.E.H. MacDonald and family returned to Toronto and their home on Quebec Avenue …, the MacDonald family moved to 475 Quebec Avenue (the house was later renumbered as 105), still in the Junction area."

lxxii Margaret Edison, *Thoreau MacDonald: a catalogue of design and illustration*, p 8.

lxxiii The AGO website entry for MacDonald's *Sunset After the Rains* states, "MacDonald also helped Tom Thomson design and build a cottage by hand at 475 Quebec Avenue (High Park Area) in 1907". The Roberts Gallery website posting for MacDonald's *High Park,* 1910, reiterates this information. In Margaret Edison's book about Thoreau MacDonald, Thoreau says his father designed the house. Since the land was owned by MacDonald, the likelier scenario is that J.E.H. designed and built the house with the help of Tom.

lxxiv J.E.H. MacDonald, quoted in *The Group of Seven,* by Thoreau MacDonald p 1, "There was a great stirring up of the Canadian ideal. The Art League and its publications, the Graphic Arts Club with its Canadian evenings (the fellows all singing canoe songs and ranged like canoe-men on the benches), and the half-hour compositions we made on Canadian subjects."

lxxv Albert Robson, *Tom Thomson,* p 5. Robson estimates the meeting took place in 1908. It would have been late 1908.

lxxvi Jamie Bradburn, "Vintage Toronto Ads: Brown Betty Tea Rooms", torontoist.com, January 7, 2015, "When the restaurant was evicted around 1910 and forced to move one door east, club members contemplated drastic action to maintain a convenient food source. "This took away our means of support and compelled us to have trays fetched downstairs and up again from next door," journalist Augustus Bridle recounted a decade later, "till one day the Secretary began to hammer the stairway wall with a view to having a hole punched through for better service—and before the hole could be made the landlord kicked us casually into the street."

lxxvii S.H.F. Kemp, "A Recollection of Tom Thomson" reprinted in William T. Little, *The Tom Thomson Mystery,* originally copied by Blodwen Davies in 1955 from a manuscript by Kemp.

lxxviii Thoreau MacDonald's childhood journals are in John Sabean's *A Boy All Spirit.*

lxxix S.H.F. Kemp, "A Recollection of Tom Thomson", 1955 recalls that Tom was good at the elaborate shading machine known as the Ben Day. "By it a considerable variety of shading can be put either on a drawing or a plate for reproduction by the process known as photo engraving." P 175 of Kemp's manuscript copied by Blodwen Davies and reprinted in William T. Little's *The Tom Thomson Mystery.*

lxxx *The Last Best West* is a book available on bac-lac.gc.ca*.* The "Last Best West" was also a program developed by the Immigration Branch of the Canadian Department of the Interior from 1896 until WWI. It produced brochures, pamphlets, and atlases to encourage farmers to settle in western Canada.

lxxxi Tom Thomson's nephew Gibson Henry (Thomas James Gibson Henry 1912–1994) was one of the first Canadian meteorologists to use computers and computer models in meteorological research.

lxxxii "G.T.R. Station Staff Photo" *Forester,* Huntsville, Thursday, July 26, 1906.

lxxxiii "Myron Butman" in the U-M Library Digital Collections. Great Lakes Maritime Database.

lxxxiv Research Committee of Muskoka Pioneer Village, *Huntsville: pictures from the past,* p. 115.

lxxxv *1911 Census of Canada*, Toronto Centre, Sub-District 21 – Ward three, Library and Archives Canada.

lxxxvi Paul Dulmage, "Toronto Shrine to Receive Donation", *The Sun,* Swift Current, Friday, September 6, 1963, p. 6. (source from Linda Morita, Archivist at McMichael Canadian Art Collection).

where he sailed the Great Lakes. In moving to Muskoka he maintained his love of sailing by supplying on the local steamers while, at the same time, doing some purchasing for the local tannery." *Huntsville: pictures from the past,* Research Committee of the Muskoka Pioneer Village, p 115.

lxxxviii Edgar Burke appears on the *1911 Census of Canada* in Calgary as a Civil Engineer for the C.N.R.

lxxxix Matilda Burke died January 28, 1959; her son Edgar attended the funeral. An undated article from a vertical file in the Huntsville Library, Muskoka Room, titled "Family Faces of Yesteryear" says, "she was among those early settlers who filled a goodly portion of her life in looking after those less privileged than herself ... and became beloved by many Huntsville citizens."

xc Paul Dulmage, "Toronto Shrine to Receive Donation", *The Sun,* Swift Current, Friday September 6, 1963. Thanks to Linda Morita, Archivist McMichael Canadian Art Collection.

xci Harry Jackson is known by an incredible variety of names. Ben Jackson, H.B. Jackson, H. Ben Jackson. I decided to go with the name in his 1953 obituary.

xcii The *Toronto City Directory* of 1912 has Harry Jackson at 277 Jarvis Street.

xciii Thomas Henry Marten (1880–1950) was an artist who worked at Grip Limited.

xciv "Services Are Held for Harry Jackson", *Monroe Evening News,* July 5, 1953. From Monroe County Historical Museum, Monroe, Michigan.

xcv Blodwen Davies, *Tom Thomson: the story of a man who looked for beauty and for truth in the wilderness*, p. 36, "His friends gave him a pack sack and a Dutch oven and in May sent him off, full of anticipation ...."

xcvi Ottelyn Addison, *Early Days in Algonquin Park*, p. 79 "Tom Thomson and H.B. Jackson arrived in the Park in May 1912 for a canoe trip. Shannon Fraser watched them load their canoe at the Mowat dock in the teeth of a high wind and suggested it might be wise to stay overnight with him. There may have been other unofficial guests before Fraser got around to advertising his place as a fishing lodge in 1913."

xcvii Ibid, *Early Days in Algonquin Park,* p 123.

xcviii Ibid, *Early Days in Algonquin Park,* p 133, "Berry picking was the biggest summer undertaking. There were plenty of berry patches, the aftermath of lumbering or a regrowth area after forest fires."

xcix Harry B. Jackson letter to Blodwen Davies, May 5, 1931, Library and Archives Canada.

c William Smithson Broadhead's letters to his parents are in the City of Sheffield Archives. For more information go to www.sheffield.gov.uk/archives .

ci Rolph-Clark-Stone Fonds (P096) is at the McCord Museum. When Broadhead worked there it was Rolph & Clark Limited.

cii Jane Billinghurst, *Grey Owl: the many faces of Archie Belaney,* p. 28, "Archie met Marie one day when he was having an early breakfast at the boarding house. She came into the dining room with a tray full of cutlery, which she proceeded to throw up into the air. Archie joined in her laughter as it fell to the floor."

ciii Factors were persons acting as mercantile agents for the Hudson Bay Company. The company had 25 chief factors and 28 chief traders who shared in the profits of the company.

civ "Local Man's Experience in Northern Wilds", *Owen Sound Sun,* September 27, 1912, *West Wind* website.

cv Louisa Thomson Henry letter to Blodwen Davies, March 11, 1931, *West Wind* website.

cvi Tom Thomson to Dr. John McRuer, October 17, 1912, "All the fishing there is up in the north country is pike and they are so thick there is no fun in it." *West Wind* website.

cvii Blodwen Davies, *Tom Thomson*, p 40, "MacCallum's friend Colonel Mason and two nephews found Tom and Broadhead salvaging sketches."

cviii Albert Robson, *Tom Thomson,* p 7.

cix Donald B. Smith, *From the Land of Shadows: The Making of Grey Owl*, p 189, Hugh Eayrs recounted, "The lecture [in the Throne Room with two 35mm projectors] was an enormous success. Everybody was very interested and when it was over the King and both Queens and the Princesses spoke to Grey Owl for nearly half an hour and finally invited us to have tea at the Palace, which we did."

cx Donald B. Smith, *From the Land of Shadows: The Making of Grey Owl,* p 36. Talking about Belaney's lost autobiographical manuscript from 1916 or 1917, Smith writes, "... the tattered exercise book contained a vivid account of a young immigrant's experiences "working in a large department store of the biggest city in Ontario" selling men's ties and other "gents furnishings" across the counter."

cxi The story of Archie living with the Guppy family is told in *Bill Guppy: King of the Woodsmen,* available free online at our roots: Canada's Local Histories Online. Chapter Four is on Grey Owl.

cxii Julia Luttrell, "Grey Owl – Anatomy of a Myth", *Northern Stories,* northernontario.org/NorthernStories/GreyOwlJL.htm.

cxiii Archie and Angele had two children. Agnes in 1911 and Flora in 1925. Doug Mackey, "The Angele Project" in *Heritage Perspective*, June 2, 2006, provides family context for Agnes Belaney-Lalonde.

cxiv Joan Luttrell, "Grey Owl – Anatomy of a Myth", claims that the Indians were never deceived. "How could anyone ever mistake him for an Indian. Certainly the Indians never did, although I suspect they enjoyed his act immensely."

cxv Donald B. Smith, *From the Land of Shadows: the making of Grey Owl,* p. 48, "At home they [the Legace family] had a gramophone record player, the kind that had to be wound up with a crank. Archie would select a record he liked and play it over and over until he knew it by heart. Then he would practise on the piano until he could play the piece by ear. He played the piano at the dances."

cxvi Joan Murray, "Chronology, 1912", in Dennis Reid ed., *Tom Thomson*, p 311.

cxvii Archie Belaney haled from Hastings and William Broadhead from Sheffield.

cxviii Doug Mackey, "Two artists, two Kindred spirits", *The Cottage Times,* September 2002, also at pastforward.ca/perspectives/columns/sep_2002.htm.

cxix Jane Billinghurst, *The Many Faces of Grey Owl,* p 28.

cxx Donald B. Smith, Jane Billinghurst, Lovat Dickson and Irene Gordon are Grey Owl biographers.

cxxiWilliam Arthur Deacon, (1890–1977) "Knew Famous Tom Thomson as Good Doughnut Maker", Owen Sound, *Sun Times*, November 1936. This article derived from *Mail and Empire*, "Famed Canvases Found in Cabin", November 9, 1936. As literary editor of *Mail and Empire* (1928–36), and *Globe and Mail* (1936-60), Deacon was Canada's best-known bookman.

cxxii Nathanael Reed, *Goodbyes Along the Way: The People and Stories of Mattagami First Nation,* pp 62–63.

cxxiii Donald B. Smith, *From the Land of Shadows*, p 49, "Frank Coryell, a Toronto businessman, hired Archie as a guide in 1913 after the fire ranging season ended .... On their 10 day hunting trip in the Mississagi Forest Reserve, Archie told him about 'fighting Yaqui Indians in New Mexico'....That winter Archie came south and called on Frank Coryell at the furniture store he managed in Toronto."

cxxiv William Arthur Deacon, "Knew Famous Tom Thomson as Good Doughnut Maker", Owen Sound, *Sun Times*, November 1936.

cxxv The mountain painting is still undergoing the authentication process but has already withstood rigorous scientific testing and screening by art historians.

cxxvi Blodwen Davies, Tom Thomson, p 4.

cxxvii Franklin Carmichael 1915 letter to Ada Went on the *West Wind* website.

cxxviii Franklin Carmichael had a studio at 49 Murray Street in 1912 and at 68 Gloucester Street in 1913.

cxxix Megan Bice, *Light and Shadow: The Work of Franklin Carmichael,* p 10, "The friendship [Franklin Carmichael and Fred Haines] endured; the cousins continued to play music, to discuss art and to sketch together throughout their lives."

cxxx Fred Haines and George Chavignaud had homes in Meadowvale. A.J. Casson, Owen Staples, John Beatty and A.Y. Jackson came to paint there. From Allen Emerson's memories, "From the time I was a little boy, I can remember the artists coming out to Meadowvale to paint the mill, the barn, the mill house and other beautiful historic buildings in the area, including the Apple Tree Inn, the cottage, flats and the dam....On summer days we would often hear a terrible clammering [sic] and clattering outside the house and look out to find that there was a row of cars parked on the grass outside the fence and half a dozen people would be setting up their easels ..." mississauga.ca/file/COM/9661_MeadowvaleBook_PartThree.pdf

cxxxi M.O.Hammond, a photographer and member of the Arts and Letters Club photographed Meadowvale Village and also Tom Thomson (Archives of Ontario); Hammond visited Tom in the Shack in December 10, 1915, "Tom, whom I now first met, is a medium, well built chap, with a clean face and the hard hands of the woodsman. But, the place was awfully bare. He and Lismer work together and both are about bankrupt. There was no fire in the stove and he explained it did not draw well for lack of enough pipe. But I perceive the real reason is no money for fuel." Quotation is from the *West Wind* website, "Life in the Shack, 1915".

cxxxii Rev. Canon Richard Waddilove Eustace Greene (1848–1934) had served on the staff of St. James' Cathedral in Toronto and had also worked as a city missionary in St. Louis, Missouri before arriving in Orillia in 1888. The city of Orillia Hall of Fame website says, "A painter, he [Greene] was the centre of the artistic life of the town, encouraging young artists, including Franklin Carmichael, in their work."

cxxxiii The National Gallery of Canada holds the Library of Franklin Carmichael which includes 580 books, exhibition catalogues, periodicals and technical manuals.

cxxxiv William Brodie quoted in Louise Hertzberg's *A Pocketful of Galls,* p 48.

cxxxv John Hartman in *W.J. Wood: Paintings and Graphics,* p. 17, indicates that Wood had been a carriage burnisher and painter in the Midland dockyards.

cxxxvi John Hartman, *W.J. Wood: Paintings and Graphics*, p. 48. Hartman references a 1909 letter of Wood to his wife Jesse.

cxxxvii W.J. Wood letter is in File #1 *W.J. Wood Collection,* Art Gallery of Ontario.

cxxxviii John McLeish, *September Gale: A study of Arthur Lismer of the Group of Seven*, Dent and Sons 1956, pp 49-50.

cxxxix Lawren Harris, *The Story of the Group of Seven,* excerpt from "Move to the Shack, 1915", *West Wind* website.

cxl Franklin Carmichael letter dated Bolton, May 25, 1915, in the McMichael Canadian Art Collection Archives.

cxli Phoebe Street Public School, 33 Phoebe Street, 1855–1905, destroyed by fire. Opened 1907 as Ogden P.S. from website *For King and Country: a project to transcribe the war memorials in Toronto schools.*

cxlii Samuel Beatty was a skilled housepainter and wood grainer.

cxliii Caroline Cornock's family was from Cardwell County an electoral district established in 1867 and comprised of four townships, Albion, Caledon, Mono and Adjala. Cardwell disappeared as an electoral district in 1903.

cxliv Dorothy Hoover, *J.W. Beatty,* p 5.

cxlv Frederick Challener 1869–1959 was a well-respected muralist who decorated McConkey's Restaurant in 1895, the King Edward Hotel, Toronto 1900 and the Royal Alexandra Theatre, Toronto 1907; he painted *The Fathers of Confederation* for the Legislative Building of the Government of Ontario in 1919.

cxlvi Prince Arthur, Duke of Connaught and Strathearn, was the 7th child of Queen Victoria and the 10th Governor General of Canada. He held the position from 1911–1916.

cxlvii James Elliott, "Artist's brush lacked the colour in his life", *Windsor Star,* May 9, 1981 (John Beatty vertical file in the Edward P. Taylor Library & Archives, Art Gallery of Ontario).

cxlviii Augustus Bridle, *Arts and Letters Newsletter*, February 1982, p 9 (John Beatty vertical file Edward P. Taylor Library and Archives, Art Gallery of Ontario).

cxlix Dorothy Hoover, *op cit*, p 29.

cl Dorothy Farr, *J.W. Beatty,* p 28.

cli Mattagami, also spelled Metagami, is a large region which is south of Timmins and between Chapleau and Kirkland Lake.

clii Dorothy M. Farr, "Beatty Helped Pave the Way for a New Canadian Art" refers to "Views of the World: what artists are doing", *Toronto Globe,* October 30, 1909.

cliii "Neil McKechnie, Artist, of Toronto: Fatal Canoe Accident Near Fort Metagami—Deceased Was Member of Graphic Arts Club – The Body Many Not be Recovered", *The Globe,* June 29, 1904, *Death on a Painted Lake* website.

cliv Dorothy Hoover, *J.W. Beatty,* p 15. Dorothy Hoover was the daughter of Frederick Haines

clv Dorothy Hoover, p 21.

clvi Dorothy Hoover, *op cit*, p 22.

clvii "He Was A Pioneer in Art Friend Says of J.W. Beatty", *Toronto Telegram*, October 9, 1941, Beatty vertical file, Art Gallery of Ontario.

clviii Dorothy Hoover, *J.W. Beatty*, p 23.

clix Dorothy Hoover, op cit, p 23.

clx Beatty's *Morning Algonquin Park,* was purchased by the National Gallery.

clxi Dorothy Farr, J.W. Beatty p 28, states that their paintings were exhibited in the Canadian Northern Railroad Building at the CNE in August 1915.

clxii "Dorothy Stone, Recollections offered to William Little" excerpt in William Little, *The Tom Thomson Mystery* pp 106–109.

clxiii J.E.H. letter of fall 1917 quoted in Dorothy Farr, *J.W. Beatty*, p 30.

clxiv Bridle quotation in Dorothy Farr, *J.W. Beatty* p 30.

clxv Augustus Bridle, art critic *The Star,* John Beatty vertical file, E.P. Taylor Research Library & Archives, Art Gallery of Ontario.

clxvi I went through information at the South River–Machar Union Public Library for all postmasters of South River and area to find the right postmaster, at the right time, who had a daughter who was his assistant. The only person who fit the bill was Arthur Smyth (1863–1944) who worked for over 25 years as the South River postmaster. His daughter Alice was his assistant. Ancestry.ca supplied the rest of the information.

clxvii The 1911 and 1921 Census lists Richard McGrath as a Saw Mill Foreman. Thanks to Keith Thornborrow for this information.

clxviii According to a map of South River in a church cookbook, Edna McGrath lived at 23 Hunter Street on the corner of Marie Street. She was the daughter of Richard and Edith McGrath. Born in 1885 Edna would have been 28-years-old when she met Tom Thomson. South River artist, Brenda Scott, maintains Tom courted Edna on the porch and in the parlour of 23 Hunter Street.

clxix From a hand written note in the Ard family vertical file in the South River–Machar Union Public Library.

clxx The information about the Wattie homes and camps comes from South River historian Keith Thornborrow who is a friend of the Wattie family and who generously shared his collection of photo albums and clippings.

clxxi Joan Murray's chronology in the *Catalogue Raisonné* uses the word 'may' to say that Tom may have been a fire ranger on the Mattagami Reserve. I move the 'may' to a certainty as there is no credible alternative evidence as to where else Tom was in the spring and summer of 1913.

clxxii Tom Thomson letter to Fred Varley, July 8, 1914 on the *West Wind* website.

clxxiii Leonard E. Mack letter to Tom Thomson, March 16, 1913 on *Death on a Painted Lake* website.

clxxiv Arthur Lismer letter, 1914 on *West Wind* website: "... and sketching impedimenta, this last consisting (for me) of two dozen 12x9 inch [30x23 cm] three-ply veneer boards of birch wood back and front and a soft pine inside, and good for sketching. These fit into a holder designed to carry six or more in a flat sketch box, also about twelve to fifteen pounds [5.4–6.8 kg] of paint, oil, and brushes per man."

clxxv Tom wrote Dr. James MacCallum in a letter dated October 6, 1914, "I have probably used most of it up [money in his bank account] by this time and it is just to find out if I should ride or walk back to Toronto." The letter is on *Death on a Painted Lake* website.

clxxvi The *Ravenwood: Canoe and Boatworks* blog has several authoritative discussions on Tom's canoe and the colour he achieved. See the Thursday 15 March 2012 and the Sunday 19 May 2013 entries.

clxxvii Dr. R.P. Little, "Some Recollections of Tom Thomson and Canoe Lake", *Culture* 16 (1955) pp 210-222.

clxxviii Tom Thomson to Dr. James MacCallum, September 8, 1915 on the *West Wind* website.

clxxix The Tom Thomson and Edna McGrath romance is told exclusively by South River artist Brenda Scott and has not yet been substantiated.

clxxx Dr. MacCallum wrote on the back of *Sand Hill on the Road to South River,* "on this day Thomson tramped 14 miles [22.5 km] carrying a sketch box and gun—a fox and seven partridge which he shot that day ..."

clxxxi Tom Wattie's son Gord found a new tent, packs, a fold up cot, sleeping bag, waterproof trousers and some cooking gear after he took over the Ottawa Avenue house.

clxxxii Joan Murray, "Remarks" for *Autumn Scene,* 1916 in the *Catalogue Raisonné*. "Kidd had already noticed that there were piles of birch panels ready for him."

clxxxiii Taylor Statten founded Camp Ahmek in 1921. Ernest Thompson Seton visited there in 1922. Stuart Logan Thompson was Ahmek's first naturalist in 1921.

clxxxiv *Interview with Pete Sauvé by Taylor Statten (Chief),* undated, Algonquin Park Archives. Thanks to Ron Tozer.

clxxxv In his Statten interview Pete said the wolves followed him all night and on the next day they could see the wolves had been digging where he had lain down to rest in his 26 mile [41.8 km] jaunt between Dividing Lake and Canoe Lake.

clxxxvi Ed Godin letter to Blodwen Davies, November 17, 1930, Archives of Canada MG30 D38 Blodwen Davies fonds, Vol.11.

clxxxvii Ed Godin letter to Blodwen Davies, June 15, 1931, Archives of Canada MG30 D38 Blodwen Davies fonds, Vol.11.

clxxxviii Blodwen Davies, *Tom Thomson: the story of a man who looked for beauty and truth in the wilderness,* p 81.

clxxxix "The Timber Days", Bytown Museum website bytownmuseum.com.

cxc Audrey Saunders, *Algonquin Story,* p 39 talks about rattling of the bones and step dances. She quotes retired camp cook Tom Pidgeon of Madawaska, "Half the group would turn themselves into female partners by pulling their shirt tales [sic] out over their trousers, and everyone would cavort with great glee."

cxci William Little, *The Tom Thomson Mystery,* p 111.

cxcii George Chubb, or Chubby, came to Mowat Lodge around 1915. He worked there as a storekeeper and postal clerk.

cxciii Audrey Saunders, *op cit,* p 143.

cxciv Audrey Saunders, *op cit,* p 37.

Afterword

It's not easy to find new material about Canada's most researched artist. For a decade plus, since the time I worked on Tom Thomson's heritage for *The Thomsons of Durham: Tom Thomson's Family Heritage,* I've scoured books, websites, letters, footnotes and genealogical sites looking for threads that might lead to new information about his life.

The search yielded a few items, but, never as much valuable material as networking produced. Through the work started at the Durham West Arts Centre in 2005, I was increasingly blessed with wonderful contacts: descendants of Tom Thomson and his friends and generous art historians, authors and researchers willing to share materials and leads. And as they say, one thing led to another—new facets of Tom's life emerged.

I decided upon a new approach: the lens of friendship and cooking. The "friend" chapters and the "Food Connections", lined up like small silos that proceeded chronologically through Tom's life. As the reader progresses from one silo to another, the overlap should show how very busy Tom's life was—much more intertwined with people than previously described.

A selected bibliography and 193 footnotes anchor the discoveries and, hopefully, spur on research. The elucidation of Tom Thomson's life is not complete. I challenge readers to keep adding to his life story, as in doing so, they enrich Canada's story.

Please send comments and information to: angie.littlefield@yahoo.ca
Mary Cook and I welcome new photos and materials.